Supporting Young Children Experiencing Loss and Grief

Supporting Young Children Experiencing Loss and Grief provides early years practitioners and Key Stage 1 teachers with practical advice to support children experiencing feelings related to change and loss.

Using key case studies and interviews with children and adults, this important text uncovers best-practice techniques to help children talk about their feelings. Covering more than bereavement, it considers the loss children feel when they move home, undergo a change in routine, experience their parents' or carers' separation, move settings or lose contact with a close friend, nursery practitioner or teacher.

Providing answers to the key question of how to support children who have feelings of loss and grief, *Supporting Young Children Experiencing Loss and Grief* is a must-read text for all those working with young children in caring environments who are looking to provide children with the tools they need to talk about their emotions.

Deborah Price is a senior lecturer who has worked at the University of Brighton and The Open University, UK. She has worked in early and primary years as a teacher, trainer, inspector and lecturer.

Clair Barnard has worked with the Early Childhood Project for over 30 years as an equalities play worker, community activist and champion of children's rights, shining a light on the under-represented children in Brighton and Hove, who often go unheard.

Supporting Young Children Experiencing Loss and Grief

A Practical Guide

Deborah Price and Clair Barnard

Routledge
Taylor & Francis Group

LONDON AND NEW YORK

First published 2021
by Routledge
2 Park Square, Milton Park, Abingdon, Oxon OX14 4RN

and by Routledge
52 Vanderbilt Avenue, New York, NY 10017

Routledge is an imprint of the Taylor & Francis Group, an informa business

© 2021 Deborah Price and Clair Barnard

British Library Cataloguing-in-Publication Data
A catalogue record for this book is available from the British Library

Library of Congress Cataloging-in-Publication Data
A catalog record has been requested for this book

ISBN: 978-0-367-42296-7 (hbk)
ISBN: 978-0-367-42297-4 (pbk)
ISBN: 978-0-367-82331-3 (ebk)

Typeset in Optima
by Newgen Publishing UK

Deborah
I dedicate this book with love to two remarkable women in my life: my daughter Elena Morris and my niece Cecilia Jastrzembska.

Clair
I dedicate this book with all my love to my home team, who make everything worthwhile!
Michael, Harry, Sally, Rob and Lizzy.

Contents

Acknowledgements

Central to this book, particularly the case studies, are all the children, families, practitioners and students we have worked with over many years. We are enormously grateful to them for sharing their stories.

Deborah

Special thanks also to my friend Janet Lee, who allowed me to interview her and was the inspiration for some of the advice to practitioners.

Thanks, as ever, to Maria Jastrzębska who helped and supported me in numerous ways, but specifically with reading drafts and thoughtful comments. And thanks to Allie Rogers, Sandi Fikuart, Nikki Sheehan, Suzanne Drew-Edwards, Lucy Cage and Lisa Heathfield – talented writers who allow me to regularly read my work to them. Thanks to my friends Monika and Chris Stachyra and their daughters Maya, Hannah and Tamara, and also Sarah Symonds and her children Lila and William. Thanks to Lila for her beautiful picture and Helen Joubert for her help with the cover. Grateful acknowledgement to Jacqueline Mason and her son Nicky.

Finally, I would like to give my thanks to all of the team at Routledge, who had the confidence and insight to take this book forward to publication, especially Sarah Tuckwell.

Clair

I would like to give special thanks to my dear friends and colleagues Judy Simon, Chris Randall and Alex Paterson, all wonderful, skilled, caring and exceptional early years teachers who over many years have been both my mentors and my cheerleaders. Being able to work alongside them, ask all the questions, seek advice and be supported by them without judgement has been a blessing and often a great laugh.

After many years working on our joint bereavement training, I know that without Deborah Price's support and encouragement, I would never have delved into the depths and produced my share of this book; thank you so very much, Deb!

Introduction

Welcome to the introductory chapter to this book. In this chapter we outline some of the main themes of the book, explain how to use the book most effectively and look at why we think considering young children's feelings of grief and loss is important. You do not have to read this book from front to back, beginning to end, in sequence, but it could be useful to start with this chapter as it provides an overview and can also direct you to different parts of the book that may be of specific interest to you.

> The early experiences of childhood determine how the child will feel about self and the world, and because coping with loss affects future capacity for intimate relationships early experiences are the foundation on which the child builds a healthy orientation toward life and living.
>
> (Wolfelt, 1983, p. 1)

Our interest in this important topic began when we were commissioned by the local authority to deliver one-day training sessions in managing feelings of grief and loss with young children for local early years practitioners. We found that many of the people who attended the training had signed up because of a recent or an upcoming crisis in their setting, and many of them were managers. There were myriad reasons why they were in the middle of a crisis, or just about to be in one. It might have been bereavement – for example, a parent or relative of the child dying. In some cases it was a member of staff dying or a child in the setting with a terminal illness. It could be that there was a child in trauma at the setting because of other forms of loss – for example a pet dying, parents separating or moving home. There are innumerable reasons why a child might feel loss. Whatever the reason, they were at our session hoping to find ways and means of supporting the children, parents/carers and staff teams in their setting. They were mainly managers hoping to be able to cascade our training down to their colleagues. Because of staffing issues we rarely had more than one person per setting attending the training, and we thought it was unfortunate that the ideas we introduced and the discussions that we had could not be more widely integrated into settings. We were always concerned that it was a lot to ask one member of staff to remember and reproduce a whole day's training to the rest of the team.

The reason we have written this book is because we want people to have this information to hand so that they can prepare for a crisis, support themselves through a crisis or – and this is our number one priority – include this work within the day-to-day activities in the setting. By collecting all of the information that we delivered during the training in one book we hope that practitioners, parents and carers working with young children will feel supported in this important work. We also feel strongly that including grief and loss in the normal activities of a setting or a home will normalise those feelings and assist children and adults to move towards accepting them as part of everyday life.

We are not saying that settings should include a gloomy or sad focus to their days in order to make sure that they are prepared for children's strong feelings of grief and loss. We are simply suggesting that sadness and expressions of sadness are not feelings to shy away from or to be considered inappropriate for very young children. Whether we like it or not, children will have these feelings and will express them in a multitude of ways. The adults around them will also have those feelings, and children will sense this. Ignoring this dynamic is problematic and can lead to the feelings being expressed in difficult ways and at later times; this is something we explore in this book.

> Children continue processing a major loss over time. As they grow older and more mature they will have new questions to ask. They may become interested in other aspects of the loss: 'Was it because Daddy didn't love me that he didn't want to live here any more?' 'Do you think Mummy died because I didn't tidy my room?' Adults need to listen out for changes in the child's way of thinking and to be willing to follow them in their philosophical thoughts about how things are.
>
> (Dyregrov, 2008, p. 67)

Case study 1.1

Billy (three years old) is very upset because his uncle is ill and he has heard his mother say that his uncle is going to die. He often spends time with Maria (three years old) as their mothers are friends and socialise together. Billy is sitting in the book corner crying and as you walk towards them to comfort Billy you overhear Maria laughing at him and saying 'Well when Uncle Jonny dies his eyes are going to pop out'; this results in Billy screaming and hitting her.

Reflections

This is a very sensitive situation as Maria is now also crying because Billy hit her, but he is completely overwrought as a result of her words. At this point you need to briefly comfort Maria and then hand her on to someone else to take away from the book corner or direct her to another activity or area. You then need to spend some time with Billy and reassure him. You can talk about his uncle and how much Billy loves him and also how much his uncle loves him back. You cannot make any assurances here that his uncle won't die, as you don't know this. You can be with Billy in his sadness that this might happen and also his fear. If Billy wants to talk about the eyes popping out you could say that Maria doesn't know what will happen and you will find out why she said that. You can't say anything else until you have spoken to the parents, as at this point you don't know any details about the uncle. The important thing here is to let Billy cry about his sadness over his uncle and reflect on the love between them.

You then have to talk to Maria and spend some time with her. You do this by sitting next to her when she is playing with Duplo; you start playing with her and help her to make a house. You then explain that Billy is very upset at the moment and just needs people to be gentle with him and not laugh if he is crying. You ask her why she made that comment about the eyes. She starts laughing again and finally tells you that her older brother was watching a zombie film and when she went into his room in the middle of it and asked to watch the film with him he shouted at her and told her that when you die your eyes pop out and laughed at her when she cried.

You then reassure her that zombies don't exist and that this was just a silly film. You ask her what films she has seen and whether any of them are real or not and you have a discussion about this. You also say that her brother was trying to frighten her and that it's best if she watches her own films. You talk about what a good friend she is to Billy and how she can show him that.

These are just possibilities; there are a range of ways that you could approach this situation and here we have suggested just a few. You probably would want to discuss this with your manager, and also with Billy's and Maria's parents, so that they are aware of what has happened. This also opens communication regarding the unwell uncle as the mother might not be aware that this is something that the nursery might need to be kept informed about in order to support Billy. This might be because she is not aware that Billy knows anything about the situation, or the effect that this news has had on him. This would be a good time for her to talk honestly to Billy about his uncle.

In this book we look at how, as adults, we want young children's lives to be a time of happiness and joy. This is admirable, and we support this. However, we also note that this cannot be the case all the time, and we have to allow this and acknowledge it. It can be heartbreaking for an adult to see a child's tears and feel helpless to comfort them – we make this point many times in this book and talk about some of the ways that we can be with a child in their sadness rather than trying to suppress it because it upsets us. Case study 1.1 illustrates this clearly. Billy's mother might be very upset about her brother's illness, but may think that she is successfully concealing this from Billy in order not to upset him and because he is so young. In fact, he does know that she's upset and has overheard something of what this is about. Because he doesn't know all of the details and hasn't been properly informed, he is alone and confused in his sadness. Billy's mother thinks that she is helping him by keeping him away from the situation, so she thinks she has his best interests at heart.

We are not saying that, at three years old, Billy needs to know all of the details of his uncle's illness. The sharing of information always has to be age appropriate and needs to be led by the child.

We make some practical suggestions throughout the book for how to include this work about talking about feelings within a setting or a home. It could be something very small, like asking children to make a face or hold up a picture showing how they feel and giving equal credence to sad or upset feelings as well as happy ones. In this way children feel that they have permission to be sad if that's what they feel. If we are too quick to distract and mop up tears then we are telling children that these are not valid feelings and that the adults around them don't want to see them. How often do we tell children 'Don't cry?' This might be said with very good intentions, but the message is the same: sad faces are not welcomed here. As adults we have to ask the difficult question: is this for the children's benefit or for ours? Do we want to spare their pain or our own? We examine this crucial and challenging question further in Chapter 3, which focuses on examining feelings.

When examining loss and grief we look at the wider world around the child and our expectations of them. In Chapter 3 we also ask you to think about culture, gender and class and how they affect the ways that we interrelate with children in this field. As well as that, we examine how your own experiences of grief and loss will impact on your interactions, and how this is all woven together.

Underpinning all of this are theories of grief and loss, and these are examined in Chapter 2 as we feel that it is useful for you to be able to contextualise your reactions to children's feelings and put them into a theoretical framework.

One of the issues we highlight in this book is that a child's feelings of loss could be around something that an adult would consider minor and hence they fail to understand why the child has such a depth of feeling over an issue that they might think is trivial. We also note that this expression of grief could be linked to an earlier experience of loss that the child hadn't been able to fully express at the time.

For example, a child might have experienced a grandparent dying in a limited way because their parents may have attempted to shield them from their own feelings of grief and loss and had thought that the child was unaware of the sadness in the home. That child then loses a precious teddy bear and their reaction to this is deep and profound, which to an adult might seem disproportionate to that loss. In fact, the child is continuing their grieving process for the grandparent. As adults we should have an awareness of unexpected sadness we experience ourselves that is not about that particular incident but relates to a bigger sadness: an example of this is the tears we might shed at a romantic film when in fact our sadness is because we are missing a love that is in our past.

Our purpose in writing this book, and our hope for you, the reader, is that you will be able to access ideas, resources and support that you can cascade down to your colleagues in your workplace before the point when you or your setting is in crisis. Another way of using the book is to discuss some of the ideas in group training; we have included some ideas for such training sessions in Appendix C. You might use this book as a resource to give to parents, or you may suggest it as reading for staff members.

Because of the practical emphasis of this book, Chapters 4, 5 and 6 are very much practice based. In Chapters 4 and 5 we look at case studies of situations that may happen in a setting and reflective points of how practitioners might react to these occurrences. Additionally, case studies are included in each chapter in order to ensure that the reader has a concrete and early-years related idea of how grief and loss may impact on a setting. Chapter 6 focuses on resources and how best to use these within a setting to support this work. Appendix A provides suggestions for resources.

Although in Chapter 7, and in the case studies throughout the book, we look at situations where children and adults are in crisis, we also note that not everything is a crisis situation. It is much more effective if a setting is prepared for this kind of work and if it is a cornerstone of their practice.

Our wish is that every setting is ready and able to support children who are experiencing grief and loss, and that this is part of their everyday practice. It is important to recognise the healing quality of tears and to allow feelings of grief and loss to be part of the day-to-day life of the setting rather than trying to deny them. Stopping the outward expressions of children's feelings of loss does not make those feelings go away. It simply suppresses them, and we think this means that they will come out in other ways. Perhaps this will be at another time in the child's life (often during adolescence), or in aggressive or overly timid behaviours. Children might regress to comforting behaviours that they had previously left behind, such as thumb sucking, rubbing material or not want to be left at a setting where they had previously been happy. Through case studies we give examples of children who are experiencing loss and the ways that adults might react to a range of situations.

One of the main themes in this book is our belief that adults find it difficult to witness children's sadness and try and stop this sorrow that might display itself in crying. We try to stop children's crying in many ways. We distract them with food or other activities; we speak sharply to them: 'Come on now, be quiet!' We try to comfort them into quiet by rocking them or saying 'Ssshhh'. We, as the adults who are in control, want children to be happy. This is an admirable sentiment: how many times have we heard adults say about their children 'I don't care what they do, I just want them to be happy'? Yet we have to accept that they will not always be happy, that sadness will enter their lives. In addition, we need to think about the fact that our definition of what sadness is might not be their definition, but that it is true for them.

We have to witness a child's grief over something that possibly would not affect us without saying 'Don't be silly'. We believe that it is an important part of our job as adults to be there for children when they are unhappy and to validate their feelings. We can comfort them, of course, but we should not be in such a hurry to suppress their feelings of sadness or negate them by insisting that they stop.

One reason why you might find this book different to other books on grief and loss that you have read is that it doesn't just deal with bereavement. We do spend a lot of time talking about how best to support children who are experiencing bereavement as this is an important skill and much needed; however, we also look at the wider range of reasons why children might be experiencing feelings of grief and loss. These include: parental divorce or separation, moving home or school (or both), losing a precious object or toy, the death of a pet, changing rooms in a nursery, changing classes in a school, or leaving a school, nursery or childminder. The list is long: a special friend moving away, a favourite practitioner or teacher leaving, even rearranging objects in a room or getting rid of an item that you didn't realise was precious to a child – all of these issues can upset children.

There also might be children in your setting who have been uprooted from their homes and countries to come to the UK because of war, political unrest or climate emergency (such as famine or earthquake). They might have lost family members and friends, and may have experienced great danger and hardship. For children who are refugees, their feelings of grief and loss will be many-layered and profound. As well as family and friends, they may have lost their possessions, school peers, teachers, neighbours, their living space and also their country, language and usual way of life. If they are not able to speak English or if their English language is limited there will be a limit to their ability to verbally express their pain and practitioners will need to expect non-verbal expressions of this. In Chapter 7 we examine in detail how to support children in crisis situations, and that includes children who have recently escaped from war or violence.

During the one-day training sessions we inevitably spent a lot of time looking at crisis situations as that was what many of the attendees required; we wanted to support them and feel that they had acquired some practical tools to enable them to return to their setting able to support the children and adults there. We look at crisis situations and examine the current COVID-19 pandemic as a case study in Chapter 7 as well.

The important point that we want to make is that there is no hierarchy of feelings in these situations. What we are saying here is that it maybe for a child something that seems quite important to them might seem minor to an adult, and vice versa.

As adults we need to respect and witness as a supportive presence – be a guide for children – the feelings of grief and loss that are important to them. It's not helpful to make judgements about their feelings in terms of what we find important or not.

We need to recognise that these feelings can be recurrent and can express themselves in many different ways: tears, anger, silence (including refusal to speak), laughter, inappropriate behaviour, a need to be physically close to parents and carers, and perhaps regression – for example bed wetting or wanting to play with toys and books that are younger than their age group, or using 'babyish' language. All of these can be expressions of grief – either grief for something that is happening at the time or grief that was unexpressed at an earlier point and is showing itself now.

We can also be honest with children: if we don't know an answer to a question about death or dying then we can say so. We can ask them for some time before we get back to them (but we do have to get back to them). We can use that time to check on their parents' and carers' thoughts. We can also be honest and say to a child that we are upset because of grief or loss in our lives and that it makes us upset to talk about it but that another practitioner would be able to have a chat with them. As long as we follow through with it, then this is good practice.

The more we support children with these feelings when they are young the less likely they are to carry them with them all their life. Linda Goldman (2001) calls these 'frozen blocks of time' (p. 10), and we think that this is an effective analogy as unexpressed feelings of grief and loss can feel like a heavy burden, a block, for young shoulders (and also for adults) to bear through life.

This doesn't mean that children can express their feelings without any regard for place or other people. We are not advocating a 'free for all' situation where children can do whatever they want when they want and we have to allow it because they are expressing their feelings. As responsible adults we need to set boundaries and be clear about what is and is not acceptable. We're more able to do this fairly if we are honest about our own feelings, and can clearly see what is the child's reaction to loss and what is our embarrassment or pain at witnessing this loss. We will then be more adept at judging what is an appropriate response: for example, saying 'I can see that you're angry but you can't pull the cat's fur because she doesn't like that', rather than letting the child do so because you are worried about curtailing their expression of feelings.

We hope that the difference between these two extremes – letting children behave with no boundaries versus stopping children expressing their feelings – will become clear throughout the book.

A couple of last points: first, we refer to parents, carers and practitioners interchangeably. We hope that this book will be useful for all adults working with children professionally in day care, as childminders and in schools, and also for people who are interacting with their own children in a home setting.

Second, we use both 'I' and 'we' in our writing as we have written some of these chapters together and some separately, but we both support and agree with all of the ideas and issues that we jointly raise.

Chapter breakdown

Chapter 2

This chapter looks at the importance of emotional literacy around grief and loss and the possible consequences if these aren't expressed or responded to fully, and gives a theoretical underpinning to the book, considering ideas and theories about grief and loss that could provide helpful support when working with young children.

Chapter 3

This chapter explores how children deal with their feelings, how adults deal with their own feelings and those of children, and how the two interact. In this chapter we look at bereavement, divorce, the death of a pet and the loss of a treasured object.

Chapter 4

This chapter is a practical overview of case studies taken from real-life examples that focus on children in an early years setting. The chapter will give the reader ideas for responding to a range of difficult situations, and also avenues for further reflection.

Chapter 5

This chapter also looks at real-life situations that may occur in a setting, this time from the viewpoint of parents and practitioners. It provides practical and informative guidance on steps to take in situations of crisis.

Chapter 6

This chapter gives ideas for support for practitioners and parents in order to help children. It takes the form of guidance with activities and resources. We detail how to use these in staff meetings, trainings and information sessions for parents and carers. This chapter can be used in conjunction with Appendix C, which gives some ideas for training and staff development sessions.

Chapter 7

Here we examine how we can support children in a state of crisis. Sadly, such states are all too common. We are not talking about personal crisis or experience, but rather wider state, national or international situations. Examples of these are natural disasters (such as flooding, tsunami, hurricanes and earthquakes), incidences such as school shootings, war and terrorism and, finally, pandemics and epidemics.

We are using the COVID-19 pandemic crisis as an overarching example as this is current at the time of writing, but we hope that the issues we discuss will apply to other examples.

Chapter 8

Here we look at specialist areas: working with children with special needs, thinking about using books with children and the place of fantasy, and also working with children who have English as an additional language (and who may be refugees). As a conclusion, this chapter pulls together the main themes of the book and suggests key steps that practitioners can take.

Appendix A: Book list

Each chapter has a list of references at the end. This appendix adds to those resources by listing useful books and resources that children might want to access, as well as those that are helpful for adults.

Appendix B: Online resources

This section contains additional online material that can be accessed for support. The links were current at the time of writing (May 2020).

Appendix C: Delivering training sessions on loss and grief in early years to staff teams

This section contains outlines of ideas for staff training and discussion sessions so that you can introduce some of the ideas that we have discussed in the book. We have listed icebreakers and activities separately so that you can design your own training package dependent on how much time you have available.

Before you go further with your reading

Before you continue to read this book we wanted to share with you this very powerful poem by Alexis Rhone Fancher, a poet from the United States. We are extremely grateful that she has kindly agreed to its inclusion in this book. The poem is a deeply felt, hard-hitting and personal adult perspective on her sense of grief and loss after the death of her son. We feel that it voices the pressure people can experience to 'get over it' within a set time frame, and it makes clear the importance of understanding that the process has to be led by the grieving person and not by the people around them. Seeing someone's pain, adult or child, is a hard thing to witness, and there can be a tendency to try and shut the grieving person down, to stop the pain and tears because they are too difficult to be around. If a person has suffered bereavement it can make those around them feel uncomfortable. They don't know what to say, and they may feel powerless and embarrassed. Words seem trite and useless, and so they avoid the person who has experienced loss. We have heard of people who have had a loved one die seeing friends and neighbours cross the road to avoid them because they don't know what to say. We would suggest that just saying 'I don't know what to say, I'm so sorry' would give comfort and show support to the person, rather than opting for avoidance, which can be painful for them.

Our perspective is that grief is part of life, and one of the main messages of this book is that adults and children should be given time and space to grieve in their own way and at their own pace. In doing this they are much more likely to be able to start to heal in their own time, and that timeline is unique to everyone. There isn't a set time within which anyone should 'be over it'.

Over it

Now the splinter-sized dagger that jabs at my heart
has lodged itself in my aorta, I can't worry it
anymore. I liked the pain,
the dig of remembering, the way, if I
moved the dagger just so, I could
see his face, jiggle the hilt and hear his voice
clearly, a kind of music played on my bones
and memory, complete with the hip-hop beat
of his defunct heart. Now what am I
supposed to do? I am dis-
inclined toward rehab. Prefer the steady
jab jab jab that reminds me I'm still
living. Two weeks after he died,
a friend asked if I was 'over it.'
As if my son's death was something to get
through, like the flu. Now it's past
the five year slot. Maybe I'm okay that he isn't anymore,
maybe not. These days,
I am an open wound. Cry easily.
Need an arm to lean on. You know what I want?
I want to ask my friend how her only daughter
is doing. And for one moment, I want her to tell me she's
dead so I can ask my friend if she's over it yet.
I really want to know.

- © Alexis Rhone Fancher. First published in *RATTLE*,
Issue # 41, Fall, 2013. Published in *State of Grace*, 2015

References

Dyregrov, A. (2008) *Grief in Young Children*. London: Jessica Kingsley.
Goldman, L. (2001) *Breaking the Silence*. London: Routledge.
Wolfelt, A. (1983) *Helping Children Cope with Grief*. Abingdon: Routledge.

2 Theories of grief and loss

This book is very much practice-based and aimed at people who have day-to-day contact with children, be that childcare practitioners or parents and carers. Because of this, the emphasis throughout is on practice. Looking at underpinning theories of grief and loss in greater academic depth is not the remit of this book. However, in order to contextualise our support as practitioners and children's responses to it and make sure that we are effective, we need to look at some of the main strands of philosophy about grief and loss in order to think about a framework for the interactions that a practitioner, parent or carer will have with children. If we can understand the theory behind our actions it makes it easier to anticipate the next steps that we should take.

Without this theoretical foundation and understanding of context it is possible that practitioners', parents' and carers' reactions might stem from a varied pool of past experiences: those from childhood, those that we have experienced in the context of our cultural or religious background, those that we have read about in the media, those that we think are approved by a wider society. Sometimes our actions will prove a good fit with the child that we are supporting, but sometimes they won't. If, by understanding the framework for them, we are more aware of our actions, then we have a more methodical and structured way of offering support that is age appropriate and tailored to the needs of a particular child or individual, rather than being influenced by our own feelings, individual experiences and preconceptions.

We start by examining some of the words that we use when thinking about grief and loss and how we define them. We then introduce the concepts of 'grief work' and 'ruminative thought'.

> Three basic concepts – namely, bereavement, grief and mourning – are closely related, somewhat overlapping but differently used. Bereavement refers to the objective situation of a person who has recently experienced the death of

someone significant. Grief refers to the emotional experiencing of a number of psychological, cognitive/behavioural, social and physical reactions that the bereaved person may experience as a result of the death of a loved one; it is considered to be a complex emotional syndrome. Some further specifications regarding grief-related concepts are useful here too. Complicated grief we define as a deviation from the normal (in cultural and societal terms) grief experience in either time course or intensity of specific or general reactions or symptoms of grief. Grief work is the cognitive-emotional process of confronting the reality of a loss through death by going over the events surrounding the death, focusing on memories and working towards a detachment from the deceased. A related concept to that of grief work which we will also come back to is ruminative thought, denoting the repetitive, recurrent, self-focused thinking about past negative experiences and/or negative mood, associated – as we will argue later – with the avoidance (in contrast to confrontational grief work) of the most intensely distressing aspects relating to the loss. Mourning encompasses the actions and manners expressive of grief that are shaped by social and cultural practices, and by societal expectations which serve as guidelines for how bereaved people are to behave (which also differ across individuals and/or groups). Mourning covers different customs and rituals, including various funeral practices.

(Stroebe et al., 2017, p. 582)

To begin, we focus on the idea of Grief Work. This concept is rooted in the Freudian idea that children 'work through' loss by confronting it, constantly engaging with the reality of the loss, and thereby severing bonds with the object of the grief – be it a bereavement or other kind of loss. This model relies on the idea of detachment and 'facing up' to the loss by cutting off from it. Grief work theory suggests that this severing is essential for the return of healing and the restoration to normality in the life of the affected child. This theory was initially put forward by Freud (Doughty et al., 2011) and has been much criticised in recent years. It is not a model or theory to underpin working with children and feelings of loss and grief that we would recommend.

Reflective question

Can you think why we would not recommend using 'grief work' in your work with children?

Grief work defines grief as something to be 'got over', and in order to do this we have to be challenged by purposefully and constantly engaging with the object of the grief in different ways – for example, the adult regularly talking about how sad they are to the child and remembering the deceased person in order to do this. There is nothing 'wrong' with doing this, and of course we would encourage talking about the loss, whatever it is, and perhaps remembering happy times, looking at pictures and reflecting on the sadness of life with that loss. However, we do not see those reflections and memories leading to the aim of 'getting over it'. To the contrary: we feel that over time grief becomes part of ourselves. We do not detach from grief, we manage it and revisit it until we make sense of it and amalgamate it into our lives. Grief work seems like ripping off a plaster with a jerk, focusing on the grief for a short period of time and hoping that it will then go away and not return.

Worden (2002) rightly notes that sometimes grief cannot be resolved and that we instead move to accept this feeling in our lives and develop a new way of relating to the deceased. I suggest that as adults we need to think about our own feelings around grief and our relationship to and experiences of it. This will help us when we are trying to relate to a child's experiences. Those of us who have a deceased parent or have experienced other significant bereavements will know that for many of us the sadness of death is incorporated into our lives and that we never stop missing them – the sadness just becomes less acute. In this process grief never goes away, it is in the background constantly. That doesn't mean that we are sad all of the time. It means that if we take time out of our day-to-day lives to think of the person then we experience those feelings of loss and anguish. Those feelings can be as acute as the day that they died, or they can be less acute but still poignant. Unlike the day that they died, the feelings are not with us constantly.

An example of this is that in grief work an adult would talk to a child about the bereavement or loss until they (and this is crucial) had decided that the child had enough exposure to the loss to 'get over it' and 'carry on as normal'. The defining factor here is that it is the adults' timeline. Because of this they might be irritated or surprised when the child doesn't seem to be making a full recovery from their grief. Of course, this is linked to the adults' grief. They might be so traumatised that they are keen to push the feelings down, deny them and have life return to 'normal'. They might think to themselves that they have 'recovered' from the grief and so their child should do so too. They might have a timeline for their grief; for example, they expect that after the funeral the grief will stop. They might also find the child's grief so painful to witness that they hope it has gone away and interpret any possible sign of the child not grieving as proof of this.

However, it is highly likely that neither the child nor the adult have fully explored and experienced their grief and feelings of loss. It is also possible that with distraction and denial these feelings will go away temporarily, especially if the child senses disapproval for expressing them. Our concern is that the feelings will return, for both the adult and the child. They might be expressed in many ways. For the child they may return at adolescence and show themselves in anti-social behaviour, anger or depression, or a mixture of all of these. The deep buried feelings at this bereavement or loss are also there to be re-experienced when there is a minor loss or bereavement, and to an adult the child's reaction to this might seem out of proportion to the event, especially if they believe that the child 'got over' the previous loss.

It's important to re-emphasise that just because a child is small it doesn't mean that their feelings are small. Adults sometimes minimise children's feelings or deny them. They might think that the child hasn't noticed or been affected by a loss (for example: moving house or a family break-up). Part of this thinking might wishful thinking on the part of the adult: if the child hasn't been affected by a loss then they won't have to deal with it. This might be a relief, especially when an adult is in the throes of coping with their own feelings about a loss.

Grief work has been superseded by the idea of the 'dual process' model of coping with loss, developed from the work of Stroebe and Schut (1999). In this process the individual moves between 'loss orientations' – the process of thinking about the grief, i.e. ruminative thought, as mentioned above – to 'restoration orientation'. This latter concept is focused on the future, thinking about the new world that the person is in and making plans, solving specific problems and thinking about what is to come. In this way the child is able to have periods when they feel sad and also periods when they are happy and excited about future activities. This excitement shouldn't be confused with the child forgetting about the loss, as in grief work. It's just a pause in their grief.

As adults suffering from grief we know that it is hard to sustain anguish for 24 hours continuously. The initial overwhelming and all-encompassing grief might wrap itself around us for a while, but after a time we might catch ourselves laughing at a joke or looking forward to an event, then notice ourselves doing this and feel guilty, as though we have disrespected or ignored our grief by forgetting it for a moment. In reality, we've just temporarily put down the heavy burden of our grief to enjoy a moment in life before we pick it up again.

It is the same with children, although they might not feel guilty as an adult would and more likely would accept their process as natural. This could change if an adult tells them off for this reaction. A colleague told me the story of how, just before school, she was told that her grandmother had died; she went to school, returned and happily chatted to her mother about something that had happened that day. She was then told off by her mother for not caring about her grandmother. She did care about her and was sad, but in the excitement of coming home she had 'forgotten' that sadness. One minute a child will be crying or showing anger; the next they will be laughing, happy and wanting to play. It doesn't mean that they have forgotten their sadness. It merely shows that they are protecting themselves and listening to their body and mind in an uncomplicated way by healthily giving themselves some 'time out' from feelings of sadness and grief. It is unrealistic of adults to expect children to experience grief in the same way they do and at the same intensity. Apart from anything else, they will have a different relationship with the person who has died, and it might be one step removed from the adult's.

Linking with this theory of dual process, and evolving and expanding it into a series of phases and further processes, writers such as Elizabeth Kubler Ross (1995) have developed the idea of 'stages' of grief. Their framework for this is that the stages of grief are defined as denial, anger, bargaining (sometimes known as 'negotiation'), depression and acceptance. So, for example, we might start the process by not believing that a person has died, feeling angry with them for leaving us, and then moving onto the next stage of trying to bargain by regaining control. We attempt to make sense of the loss by wondering whether if we had done things differently, there might have been a different outcome. If we have a faith we might attempt to negotiate with a higher power: 'If you bring them back, I'll be a better person'. It's an attempt to make sense out of something we can't fully understand. As no bargain can ever be reached, the next stage moves us to depression – recognising the loss and feeling that there is no sense in life and no joy left. Finally, we accept the loss as part of our lives and recognise what the loss means to the new reality of our existence. This isn't the same as feeling good about the loss or truly understanding it, because we may not be able to; we just recognise that it is now part of our lives.

However these stages – and Kubler Ross reflects on this – have been misunderstood over the years and taken as rigid definitions of the grief process that need to be worked through in a precise order. In fact, Kubler Ross is clear that these stages are not stops on some linear timeline of grief and should not be read as such (see https://grief.com/the-five-stages-of-grief/). The stages are fluid, not static, and people can access them in a different order, spend longer in one stage than another – sometimes never move on from one stage to another, or never experience one of the stages. They also aren't hierarchical: there isn't one stage that is 'better' or 'healthier' than the others.

Children who are ill

The ways in which adults have interacted with sick children have changed over the years and the professional view of the involvement of parents in the medical world has also changed. Lindsay (1996) presents an interesting overview of the historical place of children and the changing constructions of childhood that affect how children have been cared for when they have been ill. Support from parents, rather than banishing them from the bedside, is now seen as beneficial to children's recovery, and the child's treatment is seen more as a partnership between the professional, the parent and the child.

Kubler Ross, while criticised by some for the stages-of-grief theory as it has been wrongly interpreted as a linear process, has many other useful things to say about children and death. For example, she notes that often children – she has worked with children who are terminally ill, as well as with survivors of the Holocaust – are much more open than adults regarding their acceptance of death and the way that they want to talk about it.

She notes that they may not have the verbal capacity to talk about their upcoming death, but can instead use symbolic 'language'. As the adults close to them, our job is not to tell them anything but to hear what they have to say. As Kubler Ross explains,

> There are two kinds of symbolic language: the symbolic non-verbal and the symbolic verbal language. Both are universal languages that you can use all over the world. And once you understand this language, which is the language that children use almost exclusively, then you will never have to guess, you will never have to gamble, and you will begin to understand that every single dying child, every single dying adult knows – not always consciously but subconsciously – that they are dying. They will share with you the one thing they need to share, and that is their unfinished business.
>
> (Kubler Ross, 1995, p. 9)

Her belief is that we need to witness the 'unfinished' business because it is important that the person who is dying is able to tell us important truths. She also believes that the quality of grief (and this can connect with all forms of grief, not just bereavement) is linked closely to the quality of the relationship that we, or the child that we are working with, has with the person, relationship, animal or object that they are grieving for. Here, the concept of 'unfinished business' also rests with the person who is grieving, as well as with the person who is dying. For example: a child who has a pet who dies and who has loved the pet in an uncomplicated way will have an uncomplicated and clear grieving process. A child who has parents who have split up and where one of them no longer lives in the family home will grieve for the parent who has left, but this will be complicated by the fact that the remaining parent is perhaps much happier than before. So the child may feel guilty and confused as they feel that they are happy that one parent has left whilst simultaneously grieving for them. These feelings may escalate if the remaining parent then embarks upon a new relationship, perhaps with someone that the child gets on well with, or wants to get on well with. The child may experience mixed feelings of disloyalty, happiness, grief, betrayal and loss, which can be overwhelming and hard to deal with. This is a complicated mixture of emotions for a child, who might not be sufficiently emotionally literate or at a stage of their development where they can process this. It would be hard enough for an adult to negotiate all of these feelings – imagine adding to this mixture of feelings the complication of a child who is moving between parents and homes.

These feelings can manifest in many ways. The child may become aggressive and uncooperative with the parent that they live with, or with the parent in the new or old home. They could become timid and reluctant to be with one of the parents or in one of the homes. They could regress to bedwetting, thumb sucking or other behaviours that they had left behind. There are any number of ways that these feelings can display themselves if the child is not encouraged to express them or feels guilty for expressing them. By behaving in these new or regressive ways the child is giving the adults around them a clear sign that all is not well, that they feel unable to easily state this or to ask for help, and that these behaviours need to be interpreted by an adult and not taken at face value.

In this emotionally charged time of the initial stage of loss, the adults around the child need to be honest about their own feelings and reactions. If a child tells us that they hate us it is important not to react with our 'inner child' and take this literally. The child is expressing something that they know is hurtful to us because they are in pain. If we react by being hurt and upset ourselves we are abandoning our role as the adult in the situation, and we need to regain it by examining why the child has said this and what is happening for them. We need to see it as a cry for help rather than a true expression of their feelings. At the same time, there is always the possibility that there is an element of truth in their expression so we need to unpick this and not just assume that they are not being literal. They may have their own reasons for feeling angry or disappointed and we have to ensure that we are not patronising them by assuming that we know how they feel.

This is complicated and sensitive work and needs to be carried out by adults who are in tune with their own feelings about the situation and willing to self-audit and rec-ognise the truth behind their own actions and thoughts. When listening to children we also have to be mindful of the non-verbal signals that we are giving – for example, being distracted or showing by our body language that we don't believe them.

> When a difference exists between what you say and what the child reads non verbally, the non verbal behaviours is always believed as being true. Children are much more sensitive to visual communication than to the spoken word. Non verbal language is the first language they learn. The way they are held and touched as infants, expression or tone of voice, and turn of head are all elem-ents that have meaning to the small child. From these messages they learn how to understand, make sense and respond to their world. We can easily enhance children's perceptions through an awareness of our non verbal behaviour.
>
> (Wolfelt, 1983, p. 54)

The recent theories of dual process and/or flexible stages are helpful when thinking about grief, loss and children as long as it is acknowledged that there are no rigid stages and that children and adults may move between stages, travel backwards and forwards, or perhaps never move on from some stages. Seeing the stages and processes in this way illustrates that there is no current popular theory that shows an individual 'getting over' the process of grief in a linear fashion. The most important theory that this book advocates is that for some people (and that includes children), grief is not something that can be finished, ended or a have a line drawn underneath, but a continual process that becomes part of that person's life and that is revisited over time, perhaps in different ways. That doesn't mean that we can't live a happy and fulfilling life. We can be positive and excited about the future even though we never stop grieving for the person that we miss.

We know that childhood experiences can affect our development into adolescence:

> Grief is not limited to weeks and months. Young people and adolescents in particular re-evaluate earlier losses, developing new perspectives as they mature. In understanding young people's reactions to loss and adapting strategies, it is important to note that denial can appear at all ages. This may be a help or a hindrance. Additionally, as young people grow, new questions will arise about earlier losses. Both these factors provide the possibility for a later loss to produce grief that connects with a previous loss. When this occurs, some time may have passed since the loss and teachers, care givers and other supportive adults may try to suppress these enquiries.
>
> (Rowling, 2003, p. 30)

Rowling (2003) refers to 'resurgence of feelings' (p. 30) and notes that significant events (such as graduation) may highlight the absence of a parent. She reflects that this revisiting of grief doesn't always mean that the grief was not expressed at the time, but rather that it is part of a cycle of developing meaning about loss and making it part of our lives.

However, the suppression of grief can have repercussions and continue further into adult life, including the ways that we parent if we have children in our lives. That means that it's imperative that children who experience grief and loss are given opportunities to express their feelings and feel supported in doing do. Not so that they can 'get over it' and wipe the slate clean before they move onto adulthood, but in order to experience the feelings of grief and loss as fully as they need to and as a process that makes sense to them. We believe that the healing process for children can only be helped by adults supporting them in this process by being with children and witnessing their tears, anger and other expressions of grief and this idea is upheld by Worden (2002).

Worden (2002) proposed a four-phase model: acceptance, working through pain, adapting to new situations and, finally, establishing a new connection to the deceased. Others concurred by suggesting grieving, instead of a quest for closure, leads towards new ways of relating to the deceased (Stroebe and Schut, 1999).

The dual-process model of grieving suggested that most people move back and forth between two domains. During 'loss-orientation', grief and emotional issues are addressed; during 'restoration-orientation', the focus is toward specific problems and the practical issue of new routines. Individuals may have found comfort in 'stage models' of grief. Anxiety is perhaps alleviated by the belief that bereavement was a common journey toward a 'final' phase and resolution. However, in reality grief does not follow a predictable or rigid path. Suggesting patterns of 'normal' behaviour does not account for the complicated process of each individual that is impacted by unique physical, psychological, social and spiritual needs (Stroebe and Schut, 1999).

In sum: the cultural realities described above and the critiques of model-based grieving theories mean that the processing of loss requires an individual search for meaning – which requires an internal and external dialogue – yet must be undertaken in a society that stigmatises death and is ill at ease with such a conversation. (McClocklin and Reinekke, 2018)

Note the last point here. The grieving process in some societies, cultural traditions and class structures has to take place against a cultural backdrop of not talking about death and valuing restrained public displays of emotion. This is especially confusing for children, who may have a vague understanding that something meaningful and important is happening to the adults in their life but do not see any clear, open displays that show this, and nothing is said to them about what is happening. If the child expresses strong emotions at this time, that may be frowned upon by the adults around them. John Bowlby's classic theories on attachment are key when looking at grief and loss as children's feelings will be influenced by their attachment to the significant others in their lives.

> Attachment can be defined as the strong emotional bond which exists between individuals. Research examining attachment relationships has considered the process and motivation of attachment and the importance of early attachment relationships on personal, social and emotional development.
>
> (Evans and Price, 2012, p. 119)

Children with healthy attachments and who have their needs responded to in an appropriate manner are more likely to be supported in grief and loss and to be resilient and engage with it in a positive way than children who have insecure or missing attachments. Erikson developed eight stages of psychosocial development.

In Table 2.1, we can see how the first three stages could relate to feelings of grief and loss not being supported or mismanaged, and hence to the possibility that as the child

Table 2.1 Erikson's first three stages of psychosocial development

Baby 0–12/ 18 months	If cared for with dependable affection, the child's developing view of the world will be one based on trust. If the care provided is inconsistent or abusive, the child will experience and regard the world as unreliable and dangerous.
Toddler 18 months– 3 years	If the care provided encourages self sufficiency this will lead to autonomy in the child. However, if carers have unreasonable expectations or the child is ridiculed at early stages of developing autonomy, the child then may experience doubt or anticipate failure.
Pre school 3–6 years	In the pre school years the challenge is to develop initiative. Overly critical carers and blaming for mistakes may burden them with a sense of guilt.

(Source: Evans and Price, 2012, p. 126)

grows and develops, their resilience may be affected by these negative early experiences, and the process of recovering from and integrating feelings of grief can be halted and only completed later in life or perhaps after adolescent trauma.

Case study 2.1

Bonnie is three years old, attends nursery full time and you are her key worker. Recently, her elderly grandmother died after a long illness. Bonnie has two fathers, Sam and Nick, and it is Sam, who you don't see so often, whose mother has died. Nick is the parent who regularly drops her off and collects her from nursery. He tells you the sad news about his mother-in-law when he drops Bonnie at the nursery one day. The next morning he explains that Bonnie is upset by the news and has been unusually quiet at home. You notice that day that she is less keen to join in the games and activities that she usually enjoys and more likely to sit in the book corner or seek a lap and a cuddle from you or one of the other practitioners. After a week or so Nick drops her off one morning and tells you that Bonnie has got over the death. He says that her grandmother had been ill for a long time, and that Bonnie had only known her when she was very ill and hadn't really spent much time with her. He says that Sam is very upset and has taken time off work, but that they are trying to keep things normal for Bonnie and not talking to her about it any more so as not to overload her as she is so young. They're not taking her to the funeral and, although they spoke a lot about the grandmother initially, they're not doing this so much now. He says that they feel that this is working and as Bonnie is so young there won't be any lasting effect.

Bonnie does seem much brighter and joins in with the more active games as before. A few days later a practitioner notices her telling a doll in a pram 'I hate you' and throwing it on the floor. This is unusual for Bonnie as she normally enjoys cuddling the dolls. The day after that she kicks one of her best friends, who has a book that Bonnie wants, and next day she bites another friend who accidently pushed her when lining up for lunch. Her parents are asked to come in to discuss these incidents and Nick arrives that evening. He is annoyed and angry with Bonnie and is also embarrassed by her behaviour, especially the biting. 'You would think she would know better, especially as Sam is so upset at the moment. She's just adding to his worry.'

Can you see any of the theories in action here?

Firstly, Nick is clearly thinking about 'grief work' and the idea that grief is something that can be worked through and won't come back again. He might also be thinking that because Bonnie is young and hasn't had much contact with her grandmother she won't be upset for long. He also thinks that Bonnie won't notice that there is an air of upset and grief in the house and that she should be able to restrain her own feelings because of the 'greater grief' of her parents. This reminds us that adults can't expect children to suddenly have adult emotions and understand and empathise with how upset we are. In fact, Bonnie is clearly showing a dual process model of grieving, wherein grief is visited and revisited and also shows itself in a variety of ways. In this case, Bonnie has an initial sadness and quietness, which is deemed by her parents to be an 'acceptable' way to express grief and something that they can understand and manage. She then seems to have 'got over it', but later returns to expressing her grief in another, more aggressive way. This isn't acceptable to her fathers and they can't understand it as it's not the way that they are expressing their grief. Clearly, it's also a problem for the setting and needs to be addressed.

Bonnie's grief is perhaps exacerbated by her limited understanding of what is going on at home. There is an air of deep sadness, but no one is talking about it and they're treating her as though she shouldn't be sad any more even though they clearly are sad, whilst trying to conceal it from her.

In this case the practitioners and parents need to make sure that they refer to Bonnie's grief and give her space and time for it. They need to be prepared for it to come out in a variety of different ways and perhaps on a different timescale to theirs. They have to own their own grief and not minimise hers. There's no hierarchy of grief.

We hope that in this chapter you have found an understanding of the different theories of grief and how they can manifest in practical work with very young children. You will have your own ideas on how grief is best expressed and how to support children. Look at the range of ideas here and think about how they underpin or challenge those that you hold. All we ask is that you are open to change and accommodating new ideas if it seems that they best support the child(ren) that you are working with. This can be difficult if our ideas about grief and loss are bound up with what we have been taught in our childhood and by trusted adults around us. As adults ourselves we may reproduce these ideas when we are with children. Looking at theories of grief helps us to see a process of support that might make more sense when working with children rather than with our own collection of ideas and strategies.

Key ideas from this chapter

- Grief work
- Dual process model
- Stages of grief

References

Doughty, E. A., Wissel, A., & Glorfield, C. (2011) Current Trends in Grief Counseling. Retrieved from www.counseling.org/resources/library/vistas/2011-v-online/Article_94.pdf

Evans, E., & Price, M. (2012) Social and Emotional Development, in Edmond, N., & Price, M. (eds), *Integrated Working with Children and Young People*. London: Sage.

Kubler Ross, E. (1995) *Death Is of Vital Importance*. New York: Station Hill Press.

McClocklin, P. & Reinekke, L. (2018) Cures for the Heart: A Poetic Approach to Healing after Loss. *British Journal of Guidance and Counselling*, 46:3, 326–339, DOI: 10.1080/03069885.2017.1381665.

Rowling, L. (2003) *Grief in School Communities: Effective Support Strategies*. Philadelphia: Open University Press.

Stroebe, M., Henk, S., & Boerner, K. (2017) Models of Coping with Bereavement: An Updated Overview [Modelos de afrontamiento en duelo: un resumen actualizado]. *Estudios de Psicología*, 38:3, 582–607, DOI: 10.1080/02109395.2017.1340055.

Stroebe, M., & Schut, H. (1999) *The Dual Process Model of Coping with Bereavement: Rationale and Description*, Death Studies, 23:3, 197–224, DOI: 10.1080/074811899201046.

Wolfelt, A. (1983) *Helping Children Cope with Grief*. Abingdon: Routledge.

Worden, J. W. (2002) *Grief Counseling and Grief Therapy: A Handbook for the Mental Health Practitioner* (3rd ed.). New York: Springer.

3 | Feelings

Feelings are such a powerful aspect of our personalities and interactions as humans, and yet we can sometimes dismiss them as somehow being 'less' than the real business of life and not worthy of serious consideration. 'Oh it's just a feeling': we hear this a lot, and it implies that feelings are somehow lesser than our actions and separate from them. This chapter will look at feelings in detail and think about how they are expressed, as well as how we can support children and adults in managing their strong feelings.

We made the point in Chapter 2, and it is useful to restate it here, that in terms of grief and loss, adults can sometimes dismiss children's feelings as more minor than big, 'grown up' feelings. It is as though because children are physically small compared to adults, their feelings can be considered small as well.

Children's strong feelings when they are very young, and especially when they are pre-verbal, can be written off and dismissed by adults in a variety of ways: 'the terrible two's', 'whining', 'attention seeking', 'clingy', 'tantrums'. Yet to a child these feelings are very strong and very real, and they often result in behaviours that we find difficult to watch. We want children to restrain themselves from these behaviours because they are upsetting or embarrassing to be around. We may be worried about societal judgement of our children and our care for them, especially if these incidents happen in a public place. A classic example of this is an adult standing in a supermarket queue with a child screaming and crying.

Being with a child when they have these strong feelings and respecting the child's feelings is not the same as saying that we, the adult, should act on them. For example, if a child is upset in the supermarket because they can't have the sweets that they want, listening to their upset and acknowledging it isn't the same as letting them have what they demand. This is a key point as it's important not to confuse the two and, in doing so, do away with clear boundaries. Respecting that children feel strongly isn't the same as allowing those feelings to dictate your actions. You might say to a child screaming for sweets 'Yes, I want sweets too, but it's not good to eat them between meals because of our teeth – we can both have some after dinner', or 'Wow, you really want more don't you? Is there anything else you fancy other than a sweet? What about a push on a swing?' What happens after this is a matter for negotiation with the child. Here, you've acknowledged the child's upset and have also stayed consistent and true to your boundaries.

When we are close to someone we can often know how that person is feeling by reading their behaviour as we add a layer of interpretation to their actions based on our understanding of that person's character. For example, a friend may be curt with us and make unpleasant remarks. If we know them well, we understand that this behaviour is not their usual way of acting and we guess that all is not well with them and ask if anything is the matter. It's the same with children. As well as not always responding to demands made on us we, the adults, do not have to take their expression of feelings literally or at face value. For example, a child may say 'I hate you, I don't want to be with you': this is a way of expressing their upset and grief at loss rather than them really saying that they've stopped loving someone. In this case, it is the feelings that we need to address rather than the statement that they've made. Of course, this is not carte blanche for a child or young person to be continually abusive or rude just because they're feeling upset. This is another example of separating the actions of hearing the feelings and letting the child know that you've done that, and hearing the feelings and letting the child act on them – for example, giving them the extra sweets they demanded.

While a practitioner may not have the specialised training needed to fully interpret feelings that a counsellor may have, they can still be aware that children may be struggling to explain themselves and that it takes all of us a long time to learn emotional intelligence and the awareness of what it is we actually feel and want, especially when we are feeling grief at loss. Wolfelt (1983) provides good guidelines for how to respond to children, and he makes these points that we summarise below.

> Be a good observer – Receptively attend to a child's behaviour by maintaining eye contact and a responsive posture. Usually more growth occurs in exploring questions than attempting to provide quick answers.
>
> Respond in an empathetic manner. Make your baseline helping response the reciprocal empathetic understanding, acknowledging the explicitly expressed feelings of the child and reasons or experience behind them.
>
> Allow the child to express feelings and thoughts. Do not attempt to 'over understand' the child, particularly in fields related to psychological data. It is better to allow the child to communicate depth of understanding to you, rather than attempting to 'diagnose' what the child is thinking and feeling.
>
> Respond to the child in language that he/she can understand. Be simple and direct. Begin at the child's level and remember that attitude is more important

than words. What is said is not as important as the emotional meaning communicated to the child.

Respond to the impact of events on the child (internal frame of reference) rather than to external facts only. Remember – reality is for the child the world as he/she perceives it.

Respond in a voice, tone and intensity that reflect the affect expressed by the child.

Develop your skill in recognising and responding to minimal cues of the child. Check out the accuracy of your understanding with the child, but in such a way that the child can modify or change your perceptions in the reaction…

Express your own feelings that are natural to the situation.

Accept the child's questions, don't try and attach adult meanings to them.

Maintain a continuing dialogue with children about death as the opportunity arises. Do not wait or plan for 'one big tell all'

Select and adjust your procedures according to the child

(Wolfelt, 1983, pp. 89–90)

One of the main points we want to make in this book is that very young children, and some children who have additional needs, communicate and explore the world in a sensory way before they are able to express themselves verbally. Even when they do start to speak, they don't always have the language necessary to state their feelings in the sophisticated way that adults can. However, this doesn't mean that they are not trying to communicate their feelings to the adults around them. As with the example we give above for understanding a friend's behaviour, sometimes we have to look at the way a child is acting and understand that this is concealing a deeper feeling.

How often, as adults, would we like to lie on the floor and kick and scream? Growing up we learn, and are taught by those around us and society in general, that this is not appropriate behaviour and we are (usually) able to control ourselves. That doesn't mean that we don't still have those strong feelings; we just suppress them or express them in other ways.

We have all witnessed people in society who, for whatever reason, do not abide by the societal rules of correct behaviour in public. These people might cry, rage, speak to themselves, laugh unexpectedly or move their bodies in unusual ways. There are ranges of behaviours which people manifest that sometimes make other adults around them feel uncomfortable because they haven't learnt the 'correct' way to behave in the society in which they live, or they have learnt them but have mental health problems that make it more difficult for them to restrain themselves.

These behaviours are also culturally determined. How close we stand to each other, how we make eye contact (or not) and how we know how to queue – these are all examples of behaviours that are culturally defined and differ from society to society.

These behaviours can also change because of outside events. A clear example of this is the recent COVID-19 pandemic, which has made society as a whole very aware of our actions as individuals and the physical distance we keep from one another. We look at this in more detail in Chapter 7.

We could further break this down and say that behaviours and rituals are also defined by society and depend on our cultural and class background. How we carry these out changes from individual to individual and family to family. It may be that we have visited someone else's family when they are celebrating an event like a birthday or a special holiday and we see that their traditions and customs are completely different to our own. Because we may have been raised to think that the way that we do things is the only way, we may be taken aback when we see a different scenario.

It's the same with feelings. The way that we express feelings differs from society to society, family to family, person to person. Class, gender and culture/religion affect feelings and their expression in the same way that other aspects of life are affected.

Some people would be horrified at public expression of grief at a funeral, whereas others would think an individual unfeeling if they didn't express grief. This range of feelings and their expression also applies to children. Children are often protected from death and its aftermath. The problem is that it is adults who are dealing with their own grief and valiantly trying not to express their feelings in front of children enforce such protective measures. This can result in a situation where children know that something is going on that is different from normal. They may think that it's because of something they've done and be bewildered and worried.

Case study 3.1

Louise was four when her grandmother (her mother's mother) died; she is now a teenager. Louise has found out that her grandmother died at home unexpectedly (she lived with them) and no one told Louise, although naturally all of the adults were upset and grieving; she witnessed this but didn't know why. The adults made a great effort to try to act 'normally' when Louise was around and they thought that by doing so she wouldn't notice that anything was different. At one point Louise was put in a room with her siblings and an adult (not a parent) was stationed with them; they were given drinks and snacks and allowed to watch a favourite cartoon. Louise remembers having the sense that they weren't allowed out of the room. Louise also remembers hearing loud noises from upstairs and unfamiliar men's voices. She realises now that this was the men from the funeral parlour removing her grandmother's body, but no one told her what was happening so this difficult, unexplained and traumatic memory has stayed with her for many years. She doesn't want to discuss it with her mother as whenever she mentions her grandmother her mother gets upset.

What are your thoughts on this case study? It's a true story, but the name has been changed.

We want you to think about your response to this. Would you have let Louise see her grandmother's body? Would you have explained to her what was actually happening? If your answer is 'no', reflect on why that is? If your answer is 'yes', what words would you have used? Would it have made a difference if the grandmother had died in hospital? What would you do at the funeral home? Would you see a relative's body, or let children see it?

Here, we need to focus on cultural differences and how these might have influenced your answer. In some cultural and religious traditions it is normal and right that children will see the body of the deceased; we go into this in more detail elsewhere in the book. There might even be rituals, such as washing the body and preparing it in a special way, associated with this. The practice of what to do when someone dies is also generational. In the past it was more usual to have the deceased person's body at home and for everyone to pay their respects over a period of time with an open coffin.

We also need to think about gender when we are considering feelings. Do we have different expectations of boys and girls? Would we think that boys wouldn't express their feelings so much and that girls are more emotional? We might also find it easier to witness boys' expressions of anger as we may view them as more natural and a healthy part of 'being a boy'. We might react more strongly to girls' anger as we may see it as out of character or more extreme than it actually is due to differing expectations of girls. We need to carry out a self-audit of our attitudes in these areas, as they are very important when responding to children.

It may well be that you find it easier to notice the play that conforms to gender stereotypes. Just as with children, you will have been soaking up messages about how boys and girls should behave since you were a child yourself and this could influence what you look for in the play of the children in your setting. When children are very non-conforming this can be obvious too. It is likely that a boy who likes dressing up as a princess or a girl who likes climbing and riding bikes will be noticed and commented on. What can be more challenging is to notice subtle shifts such as with the example above. In order to do this you need to look closely at your own practice, think reflectively about your own views and ideas and be open to looking at the way children play with fresh eyes (Tayler and Price, 2016, p. 21).

This also applies to the way that we observe children's expressions of grief and sorrow, as we might not see them for what they are if they are acting against type in terms of what we might think are 'natural' behaviours for girls and boys. For example, we might be tolerant and supportive of a girl who is crying because she has lost her soft toy, but less sympathetic if she expresses this loss with anger.

In the same way, we could think about generational differences. I am from a generation where children were not generally listened to very much and were expected to be subservient to adults' wishes and needs. Now (happily) things are different and there is more child-centred practice.

I would also mention class here, as there could be a middle- or upper-class feeling of having 'backbone' and not crying or revealing feelings. That may possibly also be generational. I am making assumptions here, and of course there are always individual and family ways of behaving that continue within and from generation to generation.

As a practitioner, it is important that you are aware of the range of different practices and do not consider your own personal preference as the only 'right' or 'normal' one. It is an area where people have extremely strong feelings, sometimes because of practices in their own family or their religious or cultural beliefs. This is an important time to remember to respect the child's family's wishes and not to judge them if they are different from your own. Children may speak to you about their feelings regarding death practices or what has happened in their family and it is critical to be prepared for this.

Returning to feelings: we are not saying that seeing the dead body of a loved one is an easy thing to experience. It could be a highly traumatic and upsetting experience for a child and they would need support with this. What we are saying is that for children there are a range of feelings and memories associated with death and they have to be addressed.

Although this book is not just about bereavement, we want to take the example of a funeral as a means to think about child–adult interaction and the place of feelings. There are two strands that we want to discuss here. The first is scenarios where children are not included, as for Louise in Case study 3.1. Children are often protected from death and its aftermath. The adults around them are dealing with their own feelings at this difficult time and, as the case study shows, they may believe that they are 'protecting' children by not referring to the bereavement or showing their upset; however, they will in fact be showing it in a variety of ways and children will sense this. They might worry that the adult's upset is because of something that they have done or caused and need to be reassured that it isn't.

The second strand is where children are included in the processes of bereavement and adults' expectation of them in this scenario. Grief is exhausting and it is hard to sustain such a depth of feeling for a long time. In order to protect itself the mind will often move from grief to other things: adults can feel immense sadness and then catch themselves laughing at a joke or thinking about new clothes. They may feel guilty for not sustaining a feeling that it is impossible to sustain.

It is the same with children – perhaps even more so. They might be told about a death (or another event, as we will discuss) and not react at all, or they might be upset for a short amount of time and then want to play. The adults around them might be upset, startled or disappointed by their reaction. I remember being called 'hard-hearted' by my mother because I didn't have a suitable reaction to the death of my paternal grandfather, whom I had rarely seen after my parents' divorce and didn't have a close relationship with, and at the time her remarks were more upsetting to me than the death. She had fond memories of him and expected my reaction to mirror hers.

The adults around the child might have their expectations of a child's feelings enhanced or influenced by their own feelings. They might forget that a child's reaction is affected by their age and stage of development. The adults might expect a full display of emotional upset, or might expect a child to keep a 'stiff upper lip'. Even if they do not express this disappointment as my mother did, the child will be able to sense it. If a child doesn't meet these expectations they might feel that they have disappointed or let down the adults around them. Children might also 'take care' of the adult. They recognise that the adult is upset and may try and please them and stop them being upset by quashing their own feelings of grief and behaving in a way that they feel is most likely to win adult approval.

Another possibility is that if a child doesn't show the level of grief that the adult feels is suitable, they might think that the child isn't affected by the death. This might be a relief to them as it's one less thing to have to deal with at a traumatic time.

> We adults can tell children that the thoughts, feelings, wishes, behaviour and experiences they have are normal. The strong and often unfamiliar reactions children experience can be frightening because they do not have any earlier experiences as a basis of comparison to help them understand them. Even when children keep such thoughts and feelings to themselves, or are not old enough to formulate them, it can be important for adults to put into words the usual thoughts and feelings in a situation like this, so that the children understand what is going on within them.
>
> (Dyregrov, 2008, p. 76)

As noted elsewhere in this book, but worth reiterating here, adults find it very hard to deal with children's pain. We spend our time trying to nurture and shield children from pain and upset, so to witness their grief and sadness, especially if it is expressed in a very different way to ours, can be unbearable. Adults may find it easier to believe that the grief is not there and that children don't have the same depth of feelings as they do.

It's worth adding that adults in the throes of grief and loss (we're thinking about separation here, perhaps) might try to alleviate their feelings by using props such as alcohol, drugs, gambling and spending. They might act similarly with children, such as by offering them sweets and treats in order to distract them from their upset. Obviously, the use of props, both for themselves and for the child, is fraught with difficulty: it might provide temporary relief, but it cannot take the place of experiencing the grief and sadness that are being kept inside the child and/or the adult.

What we would also emphasise is that children can have a range of different feelings in response to grief and loss. Like the adults around them, the true impact of loss can take a long time to be felt and can show itself in a variety of ways. One of the early years professionals we interviewed who has had a great deal of experience in this field referred to this as 'cloudbursts', and we feel that this is a very appropriate term. These feelings might not manifest themselves as tears. There might be anger, laughter, trouble sleeping, unwillingness to be left alone, a seeming backward step in their social or emotional development or learning – a myriad of responses that could seem totally unconnected to the loss.

The place of children at funerals also varies, and this depends on social, religious and family customs. Some people would not expect a child to be present at a funeral, whereas others would expect them to be there. There's also the issue of how children feel about grief, loss and death. Their reactions might not fit with an adult's view of what is appropriate at such a time. They might want to laugh and run around. They might say that they are bored.

Atle Dyregrov (2008) provides a useful checklist for parents (pp. 75–83) that would be an equally good support resource for practitioners too. One of the things mentioned following a death is 'Do not talk about travelling or sleep. Give exact information about what has happened' (Dyregrov, 2008, p. 77) – this also provides a good opening to talk about feelings.

Sometimes a loss is so overwhelming that the child might focus on a smaller loss in order to protect themselves and let the grief out in manageable parts and recognisable scenarios. For example, following the death of a parent, carer or sibling, a child might get very upset over losing a cuddly toy and not seem to react so much to the greater loss. Adults try to protect children from the intensity of their own grief, and in doing so they might not recognise the strength of the child's grief. For example, if a child has shared a room with a sibling who has died then their relationship may have been intense and close, and the adults around them, in the throes of their own grief, may not realise this. Again, we need to reiterate that children have their own trajectory of thinking, and what seems obvious to an adult may not be so to a child. A child might think that they have caused or could have prevented a death, and this needs to be addressed as it can confound their grief process.

Children can also anticipate loss by playing at it: they might be orphans in their pretend play, for example. See Chapter 8 for a brief discussion about death and loss in children's books.

Death of pets

A student told us a story wherein her daughter's rabbit had died, and just as they were all leaving for church the little girl started to ask her mother about her pet and where it was. She was insistent and wouldn't put her coat or shoes on until she had an answer; everyone's feelings were escalating as time was ticking on and they were going to be late for the service.

In exasperation her mother said 'Your bunny is with Jesus and is very happy, now come on.' The girl asked where Jesus was; her mother said 'In the church'. The little girl appeared mollified, put on her coat and shoes and they went to church. At this point the mother thought that she had dealt with the incident and answered the child's queries successfully. Of course, she hadn't taken into account the way a child's thinking is so different to an adult's. In the middle of a quiet part of the service the child's loud voice could suddenly be heard: 'Which one of you is Jesus, because I want my bunny back!'

This is a sweet and funny story, but it does illustrate how children do not always observe the same social codes that adults do. This needs to be acknowledged and understood if they are attending a funeral or similar occasion following bereavement. The adults know that such occasions are quiet and that there is an air of sadness and respect to them. Children might not understand this at all, no matter how many times they are told. Or it might be that they can sustain this for only a short while, but after that they want to run around, talk loudly, ask questions or cry for things. It can be hard for the adults around them to have any kind of emotional flexibility in these circumstances, especially if they feel that they are being disrespectful and judged by the main mourners. It's useful to think in advance of strategies to cope with this rather than relying on the child to behave in an appropriate manner and then getting upset and angry with them when they don't. They are behaving in an appropriate manner for their own age and stage of development.

We have spoken about the importance of language elsewhere in this book and it needs to be reiterated here in connection with feelings. When my chickens were killed by a fox a kind-hearted neighbour wanted to tell their children that they had gone on holiday and we discussed the pitfalls of this with the parents. These included: Where have they gone? Will they come back? Will they send postcards? Maybe if I go on holiday I won't ever come back? It seemed much less complicated to just say that the fox was hungry and killed and ate the chickens and that it was sad but that this was the fox's nature. This is what we did, and we found that we needed to add that the foxes don't kill children, as that was a question they asked!

Divorce

We include divorce and different scenarios of parents separating as another form of extreme loss for children. This might also be coupled with other loss – for example, moving home and/or school, a change in routine, staying some of the time in an unfamiliar house, losing possessions as they get transferred to the 'other' home and perhaps losing close contact with the relatives of one parent. In extreme cases they might lose all connection with one parent and perhaps a sibling(s) or step-sibling(s). Their living circumstances might also change in terms of financial/material resources. The parents might decrease or increase their sessions at daycare.

The same respect for children's feelings should apply as for bereavement.

- Consider children's feelings to be on a par with adult's, not 'lesser' as they are younger.
- Talk to them in an age-appropriate way and explain what is happening now and what will happen over time.
- Reassure them that none of this is their fault and that both parents still love and care for them.
- Try not to speak negatively about the other parent in their presence.
- Be prepared for the child to exhibit a range of emotions and feelings, or, conversely, none at all.
- Be prepared for the varying timeline of reactions: they can continue over time, and/ or show themselves at random, unconnected times.

Of course, this is a checklist for parents and carers. As a practitioner there needs to be close communication with the parents and regard for their wishes, coupled with your professional knowledge of child development and children's feelings.

This can be unknown territory for parents and carers as well as for the child and can be a place where the practitioners' help and sensitive guidance can be invaluable.

Case study 3.2

Nick is five years old and one of three children, having a twin brother and an older sister of eight. One evening his parents gather the children in the living room and make an announcement. They are going to separate and their father won't be living with them anymore. In fact, he is moving out that evening. They reassure the children that they still love them and that none of this is their fault. They tell the children that they will be able to stay with their dad in his new flat.

Nick's brother shouts at his parents, runs up to his room and slams the door. His sister bursts into tears and clings to her father. Nick declares proudly 'Well, that's OK because I can dress myself wherever I am', as this is a skill he has recently been working on, and he carries on playing with his toys.

When Nick's mother brings him into his reception class the next day she talks to the practitioner who is seeing the children within Nicks earshot: 'Well, the other two are distraught so I've told their teachers but Nick doesn't seem to worry at all. He's much too little and not as sensitive as his brother so for him as long as he's fed and watered and got Lego he doesn't mind where he is.'

What are your thoughts on this case study? Again, this is a true story.

Think about your response to this in terms of supporting Nick and also supporting the parent. You might also think about place and time. It can sometimes be an effective strategy to say something brief as a 'holding' comment, but arrange another time and place to have a fuller discussion that isn't within Nick's earshot. You might also want to arrange to spend some time with Nick one-to-one to get a sense of his feelings and how he is responding to the situation. You might find it useful to spend some time observing Nick and trying to hear his conversations with other children, and especially with his twin brother, when they mingle at break time to see if he is more open with his peers. You might also talk to the practitioners who are with his twin brother and his older sisters to find out how the siblings are behaving.

Loss of toys and precious objects

We feel that children's attachment to toys and objects that are precious to them should be treated with respect. It is difficult, though, when a beloved cuddly toy has to be washed and/or is lost. We have heard many stories of frantic parents trying to find replacements on eBay or sneaking a toy away to be washed only to have them rejected as they're 'not the same'.

Toys really are all that a child has that truly belong to them, and here we need to have a short discussion about 'sharing'. We have seen many instances where practitioners, parents and carers have been embarrassed in social play situations by their child's refusal to 'share' and have forced them to do so. If this is a situation that you have found yourself in, question whether you would be so willing to share something that's precious to you with a complete stranger?

Children feel real grief and loss when an object is mislaid or taken away from them, and all we need to do is witness that, as painful as it might be for us. This is difficult when it happens in a public place and our first instinct may be to distract or try tactics to assuage the child's upset or anger.

What is helpful, we feel, is to think about tears and upset in a more positive way. They are just a way of expressing feelings and this is a healthy thing, not a bad thing. We often mistake an expression of emotion for distress or unhappiness when in fact it's a necessary part of a child's (or an adult's) healing process from that distress. Throughout this book, we reiterate the importance of 'letting' children cry and not viewing tears as something that needs to be stifled. That urge to suppress an outward show of feelings in our child may say more about ourselves and how we feel about openly displaying our own feelings.

> Too often children are given the following message: 'Don't talk about it! Don't think about it! Don't feel about it! It makes me uncomfortable, and you, as a child, have a job to do – keep the adults in your life comfortable. We don't want to remember our own feelings or our own pain.'
>
> (Goldman, 2001, p. 10)

Goldman (2001) makes a very important point: seeing children's pain and upset can make the adults around them reflect on their own upset and pain – either their feelings at that moment or feelings they experienced as a child and weren't able to express at the time. It's hard to go to that uncomfortable and painful place, and so by stopping the expression of children's feelings we are able to keep our own in check. He makes the uncomfortable point that the child's job is to keep the adults in their life comfortable. We might not go into this much depth in our analysis, but we can see the issue that he is raising.

Goldman (2001) also refers to the 'frozen block of time' (p. 10) that reinforces this concept. It's hard for children (and adults) to break free of the deep feelings associated with grief if they're not able to express them at the time. These then become the baggage that we carry around, desperately trying not to be restimulated by witnessing other expressions of feelings similar to our own. The healthy expression of feelings in a supported space can help children to work through their pain, and also help the adults around them shed some of their baggage.

We hope that in this chapter you have found an understanding of the different ways that children can express feelings and how we, as adults, can support them.

Key ideas from this chapter

- Supporting expressions of feelings isn't the same as allowing difficult behaviour.
- Supporting children's expressions of feelings is cathartic and helpful.

- Feelings come in all shapes and sizes and are culturally and socially determined.
- Feelings can be expressed at varying times, and revisited.
- If feelings aren't expressed, this can become difficult for the child as they grow into adulthood.

References

Dyregrov, A. (2008) *Grief in Young Children*. London: Jessica Kingsley.

Goldman, L. (2001) *Breaking the Silence*. Abingdon: Routledge.

Tayler, K., & Price, D. (2016) *Gender Diversity and Inclusion in Early Years Education*. Abingdon: Routledge.

Wolfelt, A. (1983) *Helping Children Cope with Grief*. Abingdon: Routledge.

4 Case studies with children

This chapter is a practical section that guides the reader through case studies written around the child's needs and feelings. These scenarios examine several aspects of children's feelings of loss and grief: bereavement, moving to a new house, the loss of a best friend, the death of the nursery pet and changing rooms in a nursery. Each case study includes suggestions for ways that a practitioner, parent or carer could support the child, as well as reflective comments on ways forward for the child and things to think about for the adult at home or in the setting.

Our suggestions are not exhaustive, but we wanted to give some real-life examples and suggestions that could change and influence practice, encourage you to think about the situations in your setting and feel confident in dealing with them. We hope that the preceding chapters outline a clear underpinning that encapsulates our comments and makes sense of our structure for action. These case studies differ from the more illustrative case studies in the previous chapters in that they provide a structure for active engagement by the practitioner on different levels rather than showing the context for a specific point.

All these scenarios involve circumstances that are beyond a young child's control and understanding, but which they may need to deal with having had little or no information from their adults, and hence they may 'fill in the gaps' with fantasies and random imaginings. With a child's limited life experience, such changes in circumstances can be bewildering or frightening, just as they may also be for the adults too; no one likes enforced change. It is possible the adults will be sad, anxious, stressed, exhausted, scared and struggling with a drastic change in their life expectations too, and possibly facing an unknown and uncertain future. They will send their child to nursery or school because they need respite, have important affairs to sort out, have no local support networks and trust the setting to do right by their child.

> The child who experiences the death of someone loved does not have the choice between grieving or not grieving, but the adult who has the opportunity

to care for the child does have the choice of helping or not helping the child during this vulnerable time.

(Wolfelt, 1983, p. 51)

Children (and adults) do not simply 'get over' a death or a traumatic event – recall poem in Chapter 1. Instead, they become used to and familiar with the changes in their life, their routines, who they have caring for them. There is no timeline to 'get over grieving', whether it is for a beloved grandparent, pet rabbit or the school friends they no longer live near. As anniversaries, birthdays and key life events go by each year, the growing child will mature and adapt their knowledge and understanding about life, death, grief and loss. But they will live with that death, that loss, in their core forever. One of the hardest aspects for caring adults is that, however hard we try or wish for it, we cannot protect children from life-and-death events that will change them forever. This is their reality, their 'new normal'.

This is me being sad. Maybe you think I'm being happy in this picture. Really I'm being sad but pretending I'm being happy. I'm doing that because I think people won't like me if I look sad. Sometimes sad is very big. It's everywhere. All over me.

(Rosen and Blake, 2004, p. 1-1)

These scenarios have a child at the centre. The adult's response must be child focused, child led. Start by considering how you will care for this child by thinking yourself into their shoes:

- What age/developmental stage are they at?
- How well do you know them, and their care givers?
- To whom are they most attached at home, and how is this attachment affected?
- How are the adults feeling?
- How is the child feeling?
- How are you feeling?
- Is the child emotionally literate? Can they voice their upset?
- How much do they understand what has happened?
- Who knows them best in the setting?
- Are the parents and carers being helpful, co-operating with the setting and giving you useful information?
- How can you best support them and organise their routine?
- Be proactive as soon as the child arrives at nursery/school and take it from there.
- Keep home informed but do not burden them unnecessarily.

Case study 4.1

Lukas's older brother has died after a long illness. His key worker, Amanda, has been supporting Lukas and meeting regularly with his family to tell them how Lukas is behaving in nursery and receive updates on his brother. She is very upset at the news of the bereavement and wants to support Lukas and his family as best as she can.

Ways forward

Amanda needs to find out as much possible about what Lukas has been told and how much he understands. She will discuss the loss with his family and then with her colleagues – they decide the way forward and only repeat to Lukas what has been agreed with the family (see Chapter 5, case study 5.4).

Reflective points for further action

For the child

- By attending nursery, Lukas is returning to a safe environment where he is familiar with the adults, the children and the routine. This may be welcome respite after the stress of grieving adults and siblings at home. He may be especially 'clingy' or quiet. Or loud and aggressive!
- If a grieving child is behaving in a challenging way, respond as usual, firmly and with kindness. Lukas may be bereaved, but this does not mean he is not responsible for his behaviour.
- If Lukas's behaviour causes concern, Amanda can talk to his parents, and agree a positive and consistent course of action at nursery that can be continued at home. Some adults feel that the 'child has gone through enough' and doesn't need the additional expectation of boundaries, bedtimes, routines, etc., but most children feel safer within their regular routine at home and at nursery even if their initial response is to challenge it.
- Continue with the regular nursery routine, ensuring that there is plenty of time to eat, drink and rest, and sit out from activities if necessary.
- Amanda should continually observe Lukas to ensure his needs are being identified and met.
- If possible, ensure Lukas has 1:1 for a few days, or longer if needed, and that he can readily approach a favourite staff member.
- Allow time for Lukas to ask questions, and answer them straightforwardly and age appropriately. If Amanda is honest with him, he will listen to and trust her.

It is possible that at home his need for information and stability is not being met because everyone is needy, grieving, in a state of shock and do not know what to say or do with their young child.

- Do not let Lukas become isolated from his peers or from group play, but give him the space and opportunity to play at his own pace and feel comfortable, perhaps alongside his friends to begin with.
- Amanda may need to respond if other children ask about the death or discuss their own experiences. Keep it simple: not too much detail, but do not fob them off. If you really do get caught on the hop and cannot think of a good response, say so: 'That's a really good question. Give me a minute to have a think and I shall let you know.' And always remember to go back and give your answer!
- Read through the suggested examples below and think how you would feel about saying them. Change the wording until you feel comfortable but do not embellish the facts or say anything about funerals, an afterlife, etc., unless instructed by the family. See Chapter 5, case study 5.4.
- You may not have to use all these responses in one conversation. Be led by the children. Only answer the current question; there is no need to overload them with unnecessary detail or information. If they want to know more, they will ask.
- Examples: 'Lukas is very sad because his brother has died.' 'What happened to him?' 'He was very ill, and the doctors and nurses worked very hard but couldn't make him better and so he died.' 'What does that mean?' 'When someone dies, their body stops working. The brain stops thinking, the heart stops beating, their eyes don't see, they don't hear, they can't talk or feel anything anymore.' 'When are you going to die?' 'I don't know! Everything that lives will one day die. No one knows when. But most people, unless they are very ill or have an accident, die when they are very old.' 'But why is Lukas crying?' 'Because he won't see his brother anymore and he misses him.'
- 'My Granny died and she's in heaven!' 'What do you think that means?'
- Be prepared to revisit all of the above as time progresses. This is ongoing for Lukas and his family. Bereavement and grief are not something that concludes and can then be neatly tidied away. It is a process, not an event.

For the adult

- Follow the setting's bereavement policy and procedures (see Chapter 6).
- Be aware that Lukas's family may be striving to protect him from the distressing circumstances, thinking that it is for the best and that he is too young to understand. However, children are usually in tune with their carers and will sense

when they are upset even if they don't know the reason; many will make the assumption that they are the cause of their parent's anger, distress or grief.

- It is better to tell Lukas a version of events that is age appropriate, so he can begin to understand what has happened, why his family is so upset and why his life feels so different than before.
- Some children withdraw from interacting at nursery and at home, as they are simply overloaded with emotion and responsibility. Older children may try to protect their adults by not asking questions, not being a nuisance and being aware that everyone is already upset and that their crying or asking about things just adds to the burden. Children seem to know when something has been put 'off limits' or subject is taboo.
- Supporting a sad and grieving child is hard work, tiring and emotionally draining. As the worker, you must feel comfortable responding to their questions and supporting the adults too. Ask for time out or extra support from your colleagues if needed. The child's key worker must have regular breaks, support and supervision during this time. Check how everyone is doing through staff meetings and supervision.
- Find resources like stories and books to 'open the door' to help explain to the children what has happened. Give the children the information they need and that has been agreed with their parents. Children need to check things out with a known, familiar and trusted adult. They may not be getting this at home.
- Gently encourage Lukas to join in activities, but allow time out to rest or do role play with small world or home corner resources. Allow him to 'act out' what has happened using playdough, sand, water, etc., or draw/paint his way through the events and his emotions to aid his understanding of what has happened. Sit or 'work' alongside so you can listen and observe.
- Ask him what he has drawn or made. Follow up with additional questions if needed. Allow Lukas to explore his emotions, as this will help you understand what it is he is feeling and his comprehension of events. Ask Lukas what he wants to know.
- Ask Lukas how he is feeling and *listen* to his response. Acknowledge his feelings.
- Use Makaton.
- If he cannot say it, cannot articulate it, facilitate him in acting it out.
- Children can be crying, restless or sad one minute, and the next seem happily engaged in playing Lego. The brain 'switches off' after an overload of big emotions that are hard to express, process or deal with. For the same reason, grieving adults frequently feel exhausted and may need a cat nap during the day.

- Always use relevant opportunities at nursery (and at home) in the day to day to talk about death. For example: flowers wilting and dying in the vase – do not clear them away, use them to start a conversation with the children; the same with the dead flies on the windowsill. Having a nursery or classroom pet, such as a hamster, with a short life span will ensure that most children in their time in the setting will experience the death of a beloved small animal that only lives for 18–24 months. This valuable life lesson may seem harsh, but it is part of being human, being alive. The more a child is gently exposed to both being alive and also to death and dying and encouraged to talk about it in an age-appropriate way, the better they tend to understand and deal with it as they develop and mature. See case study 4.5.

Case study 4.2

In the nursery that supports the women's refuge there are many different situations. Magda is moving house. Zainab arrives in this country with her parents, Sara and Ali, who are refugees. She is going to start attending the nursery. Evie moves into (and later leaves) the refuge with her mum, Sandy. The staff team have a meeting to discuss the different issues and how best to offer support to the children and their families.

Ways forward

Even a straightforward relocation from one flat to another in the same town is wrought with stress and anxiety for Magda. Imagine the stress and fear of the unknown when Zainab is in a desperate situation with her family, fleeing from one continent to another, or the sudden exit from all that is familiar for Evie and Sandy who flee from an abusive partner/parent one night.

Reflective points for further action

For the child

- If the family have the opportunity to plan and prepare for their move, then, if possible, include Magda by telling her what is happening and why. Tell her about their new home and show her photos, tell her who will be able to visit, whether there is a park, the sea, or hills nearby. Tell her about her new nursery or school: go online and look at pictures. Have some practice walks to and from the new nursery if you can. Let her pack her precious belongings on moving day and keep them close.

- If the family's relocation has been unexpected, traumatic or lengthy, then it may not have been possible to adequately prepare the child. Ali and Sara should tell Zainab as much as they can, in a way she will understand, as their journey progresses. Reassure her yourself, as far as possible.

- Make sure your settling-in policy is clear to new families. Does it need translating?

- Be especially thoughtful and careful settling in traumatised children. Do you know what to do? Seek information and advice from the local authority support teams, the refugee organisations and your local women's refuge. They have experts who can help you.

- Try to minimise the number of staff interacting with the family until they are comfortable and familiar with the routine and everyone involved at the setting.

- Children who have relocated, for whatever reason, may need to have a familiar object or cuddly toy near to hand. What is your policy around this? Can you make an exception? Should you?

- Enable children to act out their recent experiences if they are able to or want to. Drawing, painting, small world play, puppets and Persona Dolls all have a place in helping children understand their previous experiences and make sense of the world in which they now find themselves. Persona Dolls in particular assist with their peers' knowledge and understanding about what has happened. See Chapter 6

- Some children will be happy to talk about their previous home, who lived with them or near them, whereas others may not. Take your lead from them. Use photos, pictures and books to 'open the door' and instigate conversations about moving to a new house, meeting new people and missing old friends. Give them many and varied opportunities to ask questions, talk through their experiences and clarify their knowledge and understanding of recent and ongoing events. Nursery is their safe space in which to do this and you are being trusted to support them.

- Young children's lives tend to be 'done to them'. They have little control over their day-to-day experiences and they have to do what adults want. The only control they may have is regarding whether they eat, sleep, wee, cry, shout, co-operate or not. Be prepared for some challenging behaviour as changes in their circumstances and the reasons for them become clear and are overwhelming, bewildering and beyond their comprehension and control.

- Their adults may be exhausted, living in dire circumstances, sad or anxious, and this will have a knock-on effect on the child who may think it is their fault that their parent is always upset or angry. No one likes change, and yet significant change has been put onto the child.

For the adult

- Ensure the families who are new to your setting are well informed about local services that they may need but do not know about. Signpost them. Have up-to-date information available about where families can access good welfare-rights assistance. Where is the food bank?
- Do you need information translated, or an interpreter to help for a few sessions? Can you borrow or hire a bilingual assistant?
- Some countries and cultures do not have any type of early years education or an early years curriculum. The concept of learning through play and not formally sitting down in a classroom to be taught can be bewildering and challenging.
- Encourage Sara and Ali to stay in the session and enjoy all or part of Zainab's first few days so they can gain confidence, knowledge and understanding of how she is learning and having fun and get to know the adults involved in caring for their child.
- Working with Sandy, liaise with the refuge and seek specific advice on how to keep the family safe and how to respond to other families' questions.
- Even children for whom the move has been less traumatic can still feel lost and afraid. Nothing feels the same: different house, different bedroom, different smells and now a different nursery. Let Magda set the pace in her first few days; give her the opportunity to observe and then gently encourage her involvement in the nursery day.
- Keeping busy and encouraging positive new experiences in nursery will help the children gain confidence in their new surroundings and in interacting with new people.

Case study 4.3

In the nursery, the room manager of the 'rising fives' has noticed that Kirk misses his best friend. She is also aware that Patrice's parent is moving away. She is keen to support both children and their families.

Ways forward

A friend or family member leaving or moving away or the family relocating away from their extended family can be bewildering and traumatic for a young child, who may have no knowledge or understanding of what is about to happen or has happened. Their feelings of loss, grief and abandonment may be felt as strongly as a bereavement. If a family goes through a break-up, the setting may not be told, and it may only come to light when Patrice's behaviours and responses are different to usual.

Reflective points for further action

For the child

- What has the child been told? What do they understand has happened?
- Listen to the child. What are they telling you?
- Is Kirk in contact with their absent friend, or Patrice with his absent parent? Can they make love cards or paintings and drawings they can send to them?
- Is the family separation straightforward? Are the adults co-operating? Is it possible to help Patrice talk about his absent parent at nursery if it is not possible at home? Be clear to the resident parent you are not taking sides, merely helping Patrice come to terms with and understand the changes in their life.
- Help the child to understand that what has happened is not their fault. Raise their self-esteem: praise them and offer positive comments throughout the day.
- Look at books and read stories together about moving to a new house, divorce and separation, or missing friends.
- Help the child to understand they are not alone; you do understand and can help them talk about their feelings. Help the child express their feelings of confusion, upset and abandonment through role play.
- Encourage the child to play alongside other children so they do not feel alone and isolated. Stage-manage group play to include them so they get used to new children.
- Use circle time to talk about being friendly, being kind, sharing and including each other in games. Use Persona Dolls to reinforce this message of co-operation.

For the adult

- Direct the parent towards support services they may now need but not know about.
- Offer the parent a listening ear. Do they need extra support?

- Will Patrice have any contact with their absent parent?
- Will Kirk's friends, now living miles away, stay in touch? Do they Skype? Visit at weekends?
- The setting may play a role in helping keep the child's expectations of contact realistic. Speak to the remaining parent. Ask what they would like the nursery to do; support them with it as far as possible.
- Keep the parent informed about changes in behaviour or concerns the child has expressed that may need addressing. It is possible the child is not saying much about it to the parent at home.

Case Study 4.4

Gordon is changing rooms in nursery. The nursery is keen to manage this well as Gordon took a while to settle in when he started nursery and his parents and key worker have concerns that this may happen again with the room change.

Ways forward

Following on from the huge transition from home and parent care to starting nursery, it seems no time at all before the child has to change rooms or classes. This can be a big step even for well-settled children, who may now find themselves alongside older children and in a different room or building with new activities, new workers and different routines. This is just one of a lifelong series of separation challenges.

Reflective points for further action

For the child

- This is a highly charged time, a time of big change for any young child.
- Children who form secure attachments are likely to be more resilient and able to manage stressful events better. How did Gordon settle into nursery when he started?
- The setting should enable Gordon time to 'visit' his new room, meet the staff and other children, and spend time with his new key worker.

- Before and after the move, Gordon should be encouraged to play and act out his feelings and have his questions answered.

For the adult

- Where possible, prepare the child at home and in their current room/class for any changes coming to them; do not spring it on them without warning. Their existing key worker has a role to play in preparing both the child and the new key worker. Time must be allocated for this to happen.
- Provide clear information to their adults, including realistic timelines and what is expected from home/them.
- Invite parents/carers into the setting to meet the staff, see the space and reassure them they can stay to help settle Gordon when he moves class.
- Ensure everyone is familiar with the settling-in policy.
- Provide parents/carers with the opportunity to talk through and review the transition to the new class.
- Bear in mind that a child who responds emotionally when they are collected by their parent/carer at the end of the session may actually have settled well; they are just expressing how they feel about the separation! Be sure to reassure the parent.

Case study 4.5

There is great consternation in the nursery staff room: the hamster has died overnight. The children are about to start their day. What next?

Ways forward

It was decided to remove Hammy from her cage; she was laid in a shoebox and put in the staff room. One of the staff slowly and deliberately started cleaning out the cage and tunnel run as the children came in and spoke to the children who crowded round to see Hammy. Word travelled quickly round the nursery that Hammy had died.

Some children did not know what that meant. All the key workers gathered their children into circle time and gently explained that Hammy's body had stopped working and she had died. Some asked if she would be getting up later. The nursery staff had previously discussed what would be said to the children when the hamster died. They intentionally kept these short-lived pets so that the time a child spent at nursery would most likely coincide with the death of one of the animals.

Reflective points for further action

For the child

- Hammy was many children's pet, particularly for those who did not have a pet at home. For some, she was part of their family, a friend.
- Those children who sought comfort from the hamster would feel especially sad because Hammy was no longer there to provide that emotional comfort.
- Some of the children would not be old enough to process the concept of death and would struggle to understand why the hamster was no longer in her cage.
- Some of the older children may be curious about what happens to Hammy's body now it has died.
- See Chapter 6 for ideas about using play to help children process their thoughts and feelings as they may not yet be emotionally literate.
- Encourage the children to talk about Hammy. Ask them to draw pictures and then make a display that can be seen by everyone entering and leaving the setting.
- The children will want to show their parents the pictures. Let them explain to their family what has happened to Hammy.
- Have soft toys (pets) available, with doctor and nurses sets on hand, so the children can pretend to be vets (see Chapter 6).

For the adult

- Grief is a process, not an event. It can ebb and flow: children may be fine one moment and in tears the next.
- The children may experience a wide range of emotions, from sadness to anger to fear.
- Pets die, often unexpectedly, of old age or because of illness, and their deaths can be wrenching experiences for both adults and children.
- For young children, the loss of a pet is often their first experience of death; they may believe that they did something to cause the death and so might be able to 'undo it'. Reassure them: 'Even if you didn't say goodbye to Hammy yesterday when you went home, that wasn't the reason she died.'
- It is important that the children understand that death is a normal part of the life cycle. There are some excellent books that can help with this concept.

- Show children that you're also upset: crying is a healthy release of grief, sadness and emotion. Children will realise that they are not alone if you feel sad too.
- Be a role model. Let the children see you crying, sad, angry and, ultimately, coping. The death of a pet teaches children how to handle pain and difficulty.
- Younger children may worry that others in their lives might also die. Reassure them that mummy and daddy are healthy but Hammy died because she was very old.
- Help the children feel secure by explaining that death is not contagious.
- It is very important that parents are told as soon as possible that the hamster has died. Some will be shocked that the children have been told. Some will be appalled that you are using the words 'dead' and 'died' – they would rather have young children protected from the facts of death.
- Using the nursery's WhatsApp parents' group is a good way to contact many people quickly. It helps the adults to prepare for what has happened in the nursery and to plan what they will say to their child about Hammy.
- Explain to the parents that their children might be anxious about death and they may need to reiterate that someone will always be there to take care of them in the unlikely event that something were to happen to them. Deep down, that may be what the children are really worried about.
- Put together a photo collage in a scrapbook that can be left out for everyone to look through and talk about. Get them to talk about their Hammy memories.
- When a child is upset, remind them of the happy times with Hammy so they form lasting, positive memories of Hammy's life rather than focusing on her death.
- If you decide to hold a burial ceremony for Hammy, hold it at a prearranged time after the nursery has closed so that children can attend with their families.
- This should be voluntary, not compulsory.
- Someone should be ready to say a few words about the place Hammy had in the lives of all who loved her.
- If a religious or spiritual goodbye is part of the ethos of your setting, those values should be included.
- The ceremony should acknowledge the loss while also honouring the special relationship the children had with the nursery pet.
- If you are burying the pet, you will need to dig down at least three feet so that it isn't dug up again by scavenging animals.
- Do not rush into getting a new nursery hamster. No animal can take the place of the one that has died. Replacing the pet too quickly sends the message that all things can be replaced.
- Give everyone the time and encouragement to grieve and healing will eventually happen.

We hope that you have found these case studies useful and now understand how a difficult situation can be used as a way to support a child and understand the complex emotions that they will be experiencing. The main objective here is to try to encourage the child to express their emotions, supported by a caring adult. We also want to stress that if a child defines a situation as important to them (for example, the loss of a beloved toy), it is important and needs to be taken seriously by the adults around them.

Key ideas from this chapter

- Think about how you first found out about death, someone dying. How old were you? What were you told? Who told you?

- How would you tell a child? Would you do it differently from your own experiences?

- Practice using the words 'dead' and 'dying'. Do not say Grandad has 'passed away' or 'we've lost Grandad'. It is heartbreaking watching a three-year-old search for their Grandad: 'He must be somewhere. I can find him!' The worst thing to say is 'Nana has gone to sleep'. This can frighten children and lead to insomnia or misplaced expectations: most people eventually wake up, so why not Nana?

- Be prepared to have a whole nursery approach to the death of the nursery hamster, or other pet. See case study 4.5.

- Tears are a natural and healthy release from upset, stress and overwhelming feelings of sadness, loss and grief. If a child in your care cries and you do too, it shows them their feelings are valid – you feel the same as they do.

- However, if you feel overwhelmed in the session, take a brief time-out and get cover from a colleague. Being with a grieving child is tiring and emotionally exhausting. We each have our own histories and experiences of bereavement and grief that we carry around, and it is understandable (and only human) to be caught up in it sometimes.

- Children with special needs can be especially vulnerable at times of change and following a loss. Extra time and care must be taken to plan and communicate well with them, their parents/carers and specialist professionals.

- Adults who make plans to relocate, flee the country or move out of the refuge into a safe city are dealing with important and life-changing decisions and may feel they have no other option if they want to survive. This frequently means the children have no say and may have little understanding of what is happening or is going to happen next. They are living in circumstances beyond their control. Children do not yet have all the words or tools to ask questions or to deal with their feelings. Life for refugee children, in transit, is bewildering and terrifying.

- Nursery should be a safe place for them to be free to be a child, act their age, let off steam, laugh, cry, ask questions and act things out. We need to accommodate children's sad feelings and big emotions. Everything they are used to has either gone or been replaced with something they do not know or understand and are not yet familiar with.

- There is no 'one size fits all' when dealing with feelings and emotions, grief, and loss. All are valid, all are relevant.

- Everyone, young or old, responds differently, and on different timescales, depending on their life experiences and the opportunities they have had to talk about things and cope with change.

- We all need to have our feelings recognised, acknowledged and validated, and then be helped to understand and deal with these emotions.

- Try to imagine how the lost and sad child is feeling and respond kindly.

- We remember the story of a grandparent who, when she took her three-year-old grandchild back to nursery after the death of the child's mum (her daughter), was greeted at the door with, 'No! No! That will not do! We only have smiley faces in this nursery.'

References

Rosen, M., & Blake, Q. (2004) *The Sad Book*. London: Walker Books.
Wolfelt, A. (1983) *Helping Children Cope with Grief*. Abingdon: Routledge.

5   Case studies with adults

In this chapter we look at six case studies that have as their basis real-life situations we have assisted with that might occur in a pre-school or primary setting. Our emphasis here is on a day care environment, but we hope that parents and carers will find these situations informative as well.

A large part of working with children is working with other adults. By this we mean colleagues, managers, parents/carers and other early years professionals, such as OFSTED, speech and language specialists, counsellors, healthcare professionals and social workers, amongst others. It is so important that an early years practitioner is able to communicate clearly with these adults as well as with the children. The case studies we present here look at a range of real-life scenarios where sensitive and careful communication is key in handling a difficult situation. All of these situations are a result of death, rather than loss more generally. We wanted to show how early years practitioners react and take forward good practice even in the most extreme circumstances. In all of these stories the needs of the family and the child are paramount.

> A kindergarten should have an emergency plan that details the procedures to be followed in the event of a death, but also for deaths that happen away from the kindergarten or other deaths that affect or make a strong impression on several children, including events which attract wide media coverage. By making crises and death a theme for a planning day [see Appendix C for training ideas], by preparing an action plan and by planning who does what and when the kindergarten will be better prepared if the worst should happen.
>
> (Dyregrov, 2008, p. 59)

Case study 5.1

A family called to ask how best to speak to the nursery when the person at the setting had put the phone down on them whilst being told of a death in the child's family.

Ways forward

Passing on bad news to family members, friends, government departments, landlords, banks, colleagues and everyone in between is time consuming, stressful and tiring. Notification of the death will come to the setting by phone, voicemail, text, social media or in person via the bereaved family or someone close to them.

A well-considered bereavement policy followed up by practical procedures in the nursery or school are crucial for organising ongoing support for the child and family, but this important first-contact person must keep calm and respond appropriately when told about an event/death that affects a child. It is unhelpful, unkind and upsetting to the bereaved family if the death is not mentioned or acknowledged. We also need to get beyond a curt and impersonal 'I'm sorry for your loss'.

In response to the above situation, we contacted the nursery immediately to support them so they could interact more confidently with the bereaved family. The volunteer who had answered the phone initially (another lesson to be learned there) had been moved to 'other duties'. Realising what had happened, the manager called the child's family and apologised.

Not knowing how to respond or what to say is usual with unexpected or shocking news. It is very common for people to cross the road or say nothing about the death if they cannot avoid the bereaved person. Bereaved people feel invisible and defeated by such clumsy and unkind responses. Most folk do not mean any harm; they are frightened of saying the wrong thing, making it worse or making someone cry. But the worst has already happened: someone they care about has died.

Nothing can change the loss, but someone acknowledging it – saying something, anything – is a comfort and a first step on the long road to acceptance. In our experience, it is helpful to read through some of the responses given below: make a note of those that sound meaningful to you and add your own to the list. It is also useful for the staff team to think this through and talk about it with each other beforehand so when the family return to the setting the staff don't avoid speaking to them – something that in our experience does happen.

Some of these responses work better in person; some in a card or by phone; some are better for a sudden, unexpected death; some after a long illness.

- My deepest sympathies to you and your family.
- I am so sorry to hear that Frank has died.
- I am stunned with this news; I am so sorry to hear about Joan.
- I am so sorry. Our hearts go out to you all.
- Your dad was a lovely person who will be deeply missed, especially at the nursery nativity.
- I don't know what to say. This is such an awful time for you.
- We are all so sad to hear about Davinder. I cannot imagine how you are feeling right now, and I won't pretend to know the loss you are experiencing.
- This is such a tragedy; I cannot believe it.
- I am so sorry about your sister. It is a difficult time and must so hard for you all.
- Please accept our condolences on the death of your father. You are all in our thoughts.
- I have just heard about Pippa. What a dreadful shock this must be.

It is best to be honest. If you are at a loss for words, say so. Once the ice is broken, it should become easier. Whoever first speaks with the bereaved family should ask what information the family would like the nursery/school to share. Some are too raw with their own shock and grief to know what is best at the time; others readily give permission for the information to be shared. Follow your information-sharing protocols. This is personal, sensitive information and once it is shared it can have a life of its own.

In some instances, such as when a family is bereaved through murder or suicide, the police and other services will be involved, details may not be forthcoming and it may not be appropriate to share. In this instance, telling colleagues and the wider community there has been a sudden, unexpected death is all that is needed. However, with the ubiquitous use of social media, and the prevalence of fake, incorrect information, gossip is hard to avoid. Deal directly with the family and be guided by their needs and requests: what do they want to share, and with whom? Including the family in decisions about what will be said and to whom gives them a sense of control.

The setting also has a role to play in protecting the family from possibly well-intended but unhelpful intrusion. The family's address or contact details should not be given out. Organise a card from all the nursery families or collect their cards or messages together and deliver them or keep them safe until it is appropriate to share them with the family.

Further thoughts

It is not easy to discuss death and dying. Some people are very superstitious and feel that if they mention it, they are drawing attention to themselves and thus tempting fate. This is often the reason people do not make a will or a nursery/school does not have a bereavement policy, and often why people do not think about what to say until circumstances force them to say something. Pre-planning and thinking around what to do when faced with any crisis in the nursery is important. Settings will know what to do if threatened with a flood, for example; thinking about bereavement takes the same type of strategic planning and an extra dollop of emotional consideration, but it should be one of many risk assessments undertaken as standard.

As individuals, it is helpful to think ahead and practice what to say to children and their carers and how best to support them and your colleagues. There is never a good time: it is easy to put it off, but timetable a discussion or inset training session and you can add a well-thought-out bereavement policy to your good practice (see Chapter 6).

Reflective points for future action

For the child

- Speak to children in an age-appropriate way about death.
- Do so in small groups or one-to-one.
- Explain that their friend is very sad because their grandad/cat/sister has just died.
- Answer their questions in a straightforward manner.
- See Chapter four for more ideas.

For the adult

- Ensure those answering the setting's phone/emails are able and competent.
- If the setting is disrupted by the death and aftermath and it is appropriate, inform your local authority early years or school team about the current circumstances and accept any help and support they offer.
- Read through sample bereavement policies and procedures. Write one that 'fits' your setting and is do-able; ensure staff have time to read it, understand their role in it, and can ask questions and seek training, guidance and support as needed. Try to find the time to work together as a team on this (see Chapter 6).

- Practice with colleagues saying how sorry you are about the death in the family. It is far better to feel daft doing this role play with each other than to feel uncomfortable and unable to respond directly to the grieving family.
- Leave bereavement resources suitable for adults and children in the staff room and give staff extra paid time to read through them and talk to each other about what they have read and their thoughts and feelings, perhaps as an inset day/hour.
- Allow staff time to read through and feel comfortable with the books aimed at children before using them in a session. Anticipate the children's questions in response to the book. How will you answer them? Which words will you use?
- Practice with colleagues how to answer children's questions. Your feelings and how you want to respond are personal, and not everyone will agree with you. Be respectful: learn about different faiths and beliefs, different ways of being.
- Being comfortable asking questions of families is important. There is no shame in not knowing how a particular faith responds to death, funerals, etc., but there is great shame in not making an effort to find out.
- Be very mindful that everyone has their own and varied experience of death and do not make assumptions about what they know, how far they wish to be involved and whether they can cope.
- This is especially important for the child's key worker or SENCO as they are frequently the support lead around the family's bereavement in the setting. It might be appropriate to delegate some of their existing workload so they can be especially attentive to the bereaved child and liaise with the family directly. It is physically and emotionally exhausting to be around grief and sadness for any length of time, especially as it may be ongoing.
- Give the key worker extra time for support and supervision so they can offload their own feelings and worries.
- When dealing with bereavement, keep notes of changing roles and responsibilities to support the child and keep track of who is doing what in nursery. The days will get blurred. Afterwards, use the notes to see what worked and what didn't work, and then retune your policy and procedures.
- Support the supporters. Who has coped well? Who may need extra support or time to chat through what has happened and process their feelings?

Case study 5.2

A small community nursery excitedly shared news of the deputy manager's pregnancy with twins. Just before Delia was due to go on maternity leave, she miscarried. What did the nursery do next?

What happened next?

The nursery manager took the call from Delia's partner. It was a long and emotional conversation, but the nursery day continued as usual except the manager called an after-hours staff meeting. She told the team the sad news and, after many tears and much upset, it was agreed that she would 'hold' the information and tell staff who were absent that day and then the parents, which is what Delia wanted. We had already been in touch with the nursery and given them the contact details for Sands.

After the nursery closed for the day, the manager and one of her team stayed behind to print a simple letter explaining what had happened, which was handed to each parent in person as they came to the nursery over the next few days. Putting the news into the weekly newsletter would not have been appropriate.

The letter explained that Delia had decided to be absent from work for 6 months. As she was about to go on maternity leave and her key children had been allocated to their new workers, her absence would not be obvious to the children. However, some of the parents wanted to send cards and messages of condolence to Delia and her partner. The nursery set up a message box and a 'love book', which they filled with cards and pictures drawn by the children. If any of the children asked what the book was about, they were gently told, in an age-appropriate way, that the book was for Delia and her partner, who were very sad because their babies had died.

The nursery was understandably quiet and subdued during this time. Only a very few children asked about the cards and book. Staff were ready to speak to them, but most took the book at face value and did not ask questions as Delia was now absent and they hadn't known of the babies. The nursery did not want to sit down at circle time and tell them because they knew all the children in their small setting really well and felt that for some it would be inappropriate due to their age and lack of understanding about the pregnancy.

A poster for Sands was put up in the hallway with key contact details for families to seek their own support if needed. Sands sent information leaflets for all the parents and the staff team, which were extremely helpful.

The manager and some staff members kept in contact with Delia over the following weeks. The support needed and offered changed over time. She visited the nursery a few times after hours to prepare for her gradual return. Delia asked for another letter to be given to the families who had been at the nursery when she miscarried, thanking them for their cards, support and love, but advising that once she returned to work she did not want to talk about the loss and would welcome the opportunity to continue in her deputy manager role.

Everyone grieves differently and copes with bereavement their own way. There is no right or wrong process. Some people may have handled their return differently, but what is key here is that Delia and her partner were listened to by her colleagues, supported over many months by them and her wishes for a quiet return to work were respected.

Ways forward

See above, case study 5.1. Whilst coping with bereavement, it is not a good time to make major changes or decisions (at work and at home), alter the setting or start a building/renovation programme for example; everyone is feeling raw, and the setting will be understaffed (at least temporarily). Change is incredibly stressful, and an upset that is life changing and has wide-ranging repercussions takes its toll on everyone.

Reflective points for further action

For the child

- Speak to children in an age-appropriate way about death.
- Do so in small groups or one-to-one.
- Answer their questions straightforwardly.
- See Chapter 4 for further information.

For the adult

- Be aware of how painful and difficult it will be for some staff and parents and carers to handle this.
- Allow extra time to do even routine work; being bereaved and overwrought is exhausting.
- Ensure everyone who needs it has additional support and has good supervision.
- Ensure the nursery has a bereavement policy and procedures to follow.
- Check how much compassionate leave and unpaid leave an employee is entitled to (see www.gov.uk/time-off-for-dependants) and listen to the

employee. What do they need? Will they need a phased return to work? Do they need a change in their role or their hours of work?

In the UK, every day, 14 babies die before, during or soon after birth. Within a staff team, or any group of parents and carers and their extended families, many would have had experience of neonatal death. We mention this here because in our experience these deaths are often hidden and discussed infrequently, and many parents and carers cope with their grief alone and unsupported. Parents have told us that the loss of their baby before birth is perceived by some as 'a lesser loss', as if the baby had never existed. Just because the baby died before or just after birth doesn't mean that it wasn't wanted, loved or cherished.

We know that dealing with this particular case study always brings up many deep emotions and issues. It is important to consider this and to be aware and sensitive when speaking to a staff team and parents and carers who may have experienced this themselves but may never have mentioned it and may not want to revisit their hurt or talk about it.

If you or someone you know has been affected by this, please seek support and assistance from this wonderful charity: Sands, the stillbirth and neonatal death charity. Sands is a safe space for you to grieve and to find support, whether you are a parent, sibling, grandparent, NHS professional or friend.

www.sands.org.uk helpline@sands.org.uk

Sands Helpline 0808-1643332

Case study 5.3

One Sunday evening, Greta, the deputy manager of a private nursery, receives a call telling her that the nursery manager, Mandy, died in a road traffic accident.

What happened next?

Despite being horror-struck and in shock, Greta immediately called her colleagues and told them the devastating news. It was quickly agreed the nursery would close for the Monday, but this necessitated urgently contacting all families expecting a place on that day. Each worker who felt able to do so called an agreed list of parents from the register, and briefly explained what had happened and that the nursery would reopen on Tuesday.

In the morning, the two families who had not replied the previous evening were contacted again. A notice was put on the gate to the nursery saying it would reopen the next day. When the staff met, they spent an hour crying and discussing Mandy's death. Greta had taken cake and lunch in for everyone.

It was agreed that Greta would stand in for Mandy as it was essential the nursery reopened as many families relied on them for childcare. Greta and the admin worker went through the manager's diary and rebooked some meetings and deadlines after explaining the exceptional circumstances. A parent on maternity leave from her teaching post was asked to come in as a temporary employee for a few sessions in the interim so the ratios were still viable.

This was a small setting. All parents had been told by phone or in person as the week progressed. It was agreed between the parents and staff that the children would be told in small groups and their parents would know in advance what they were being told. It was kept quite simple: 'We are all very sad. Mandy had a car accident and died. We won't be seeing her anymore.' The children's questions were then answered in an age-appropriate manner (see Chapter 4).

Some parents were appalled that the children were being told anything, but how else would you answer the children's ongoing questions about where Mandy was? As the week progressed, some parents wanted to tell their children themselves at home, and that was agreed. The older children sometimes asked about Mandy and two children compared this death with their family's recent experiences, in a straightforward and a matter-of-fact manner.

The book of condolence, pictures and cards from the nursery community were given to Mandy's family. The nursery gave a week's notice to close the setting for the day of the funeral. Most staff and some parents chose to attend and were welcomed warmly by Mandy's family. It took many months for the staff to recover from the shock and the drastic change of circumstances, but the nursery continues to thrive.

Ways forward

One of the hardest considerations was how to replace Mandy as the manager. Everyone knew it had to happen, but it felt wrong and disloyal. There were also concerns that Mandy's family would consider them callous and uncaring. The local authority early years team helped them draw up a recruitment package and, after due process, Greta was appointed on merit. Out of courtesy, she spoke to Mandy's family about taking on the role and they were comforted that Mandy's friend and colleague would step up and continue the work Mandy had loved.

Reflective points for further action

For the child

- Ensure all contact details, particularly mobile phone numbers, are regularly checked and kept up-to-date so parents can be contacted quickly in an emergency.
- Speak to the children in small groups or one-to-one and ensure they are told about the death in an age-appropriate way.
- Answer their questions in a straightforward manner.
- See Chapter 4 for further information.

For the adult

- Be mindful of how difficult it will be for some staff, parents and carers to handle this.
- Do not leave a voicemail or email saying someone has died or name them. Ask instead that they call the nursery, and then tell them one-to-one. Avoid causing panic or confusion.
- Give some thought as to how and when personal effects will be handed back to the bereaved family. Who feels they can take this on?
- Allow extra time to do even routine work: being bereaved and overwrought is exhausting.
- Ensure all staff have good support and supervision.
- If necessary, temporarily bring in an external person who is one step removed from the situation and can aid decision making, lead team meetings, help with appraisals, etc. Ask the local authority for assistance with this.
- Ensure spare sets of keys and bank cards can be accessed in case of emergency, and that computer passwords are kept safe but accessible to enable admin to continue.
- Contact OFSTED as soon as possible to inform them of the death of the manager, what interim plans are in place and, later, the details of the new manager. Follow any instructions from OFSTED to the letter.
- Ensure the nursery has a bereavement policy and procedures to follow. See Chapter 6 for further information.

Case study 5.4

Following the death of her great-grandma (Nana), Mimi's parents discussed how to inform the infant school and wrote a thoughtful letter explaining that Mimi (age 6) was very close to Nana and, whilst sad, accepted that Nana was very old, had died and she would no longer see her. Mum took Mimi into school to rehearse the Christmas play, explained what had happened and showed the letter. The class teacher was kind and sympathetic.

Although tired and a bit fretful, Mimi seemed to be coping at school until the middle of the third day, when her Mum was called into school. Mimi was tearful and 'clingy'. Sensing something had happened, Mum asked what was wrong. Mimi had started to cry whilst practicing her song for the play, realising that Nana would not see her sing. A lunchtime assistant brought in to help had said to stop crying as Nana had angel wings and was watching over her up in heaven. Mimi was heartbroken because she said Nana had not got wings so how could she look at her?

What happened next?

All the careful explanation of Nana's death had now fallen by the wayside. Despite a very clear request that Mimi was not to be told anything that wasn't in the letter, a well-meaning adult, in an attempt to be kind and comforting, had inadvertently undermined Mimi's understanding of the death as carefully established by her parents, both atheists. It became immediately clear that the letter and its contents had not been seen by anyone other than the class teacher.

Ways forward

Everyone wanted to protect Mimi from the hurt she was feeling; no one set out to cause her further upset. The class teacher should have shared the details of the letter with everyone who was going to be in contact with Mimi, but it was nearly Christmas, lots of routines were out of kilter and staff were all over the place! However, no one should have taken it upon themselves, however well intended, to tell Mimi about heaven and angels as this was not what the family wanted and they had specifically asked that Mimi was only told what had been laid out in the letter from home.

We have heard many times that nursery/school staff choose to explain death to children in terms of their personal beliefs, or in ways that they think is best or most appropriate, whilst the child may have a different faith or no faith. This is incredibly bad practice and wholly inappropriate.

If families have a faith it is good practice to ask what mourning and funeral rites or celebrations they follow and what other special conditions there are within their faith. If the family has no faith or are indifferent, then, as with all families, they should be asked what the child has already been told and the staff should continue with this. Some parents are so overwhelmed at the time they ask the staff to say what they think is right. This is perhaps understandable, but can be very awkward. So, talk it through with the parents there and then and seek their agreement about the wording of a gentle explanation about death and the person who has died. Tell the staff team what has been agreed and stick to it. See Chapter 4 for further information.

Reflective points for further action

For the child

- Do not deviate from what the child has been told by their family or what has been agreed between the family and the setting, even if it is contrary to your personal beliefs or faith.
- All staff must say the same thing to the bereaved child. If another child comments that their Dad says (something different), just say that is it OK, everyone is allowed to think what they want to think.
- Some questions are universal and unanswerable (e.g. 'What does heaven look like?'), and it is acceptable to explain this to the children.
- Some questions are easier to answer (e.g. 'Can Grandad climb out his box [coffin]?').
- If they are asking the question, they are ready for an honest but age-appropriate response.
- Do not fob them off. See Chapter 4 for further information.

For the adult

- Be respectful. The parent or carer is the child's prime carer and educator.
- Knowledge about a family's background, their faith and their beliefs starts with a robust confidential application form and interview when they join the nursery or school. The information should be reviewed and updated regularly.
- Do not assume that you know anything about the belief systems and practices of *any* faith. There is no shame in not knowing and having to ask questions to seek clarity. Families do things in their way and it is best to ask rather than make assumptions and inadvertently cause offence or upset.

- If you are anxious and need additional information in order to feel more confident, do a quick online search so you can ask the family better-informed and more pertinent questions.
- If you are with a child who asks questions and you do not know how to answer, you can ask them what they have been told, what they think will happen or what they would like to happen. Telling a child that no one knows if there is a heaven, but some people like to believe that there is, is a good answer.
- It is reasonable to say, 'We shall ask Daddy when we see him?' and call the parent ahead of pick up time to talk it through. Just remember to do it!
- See Chapter 4 for further information.

Case study 5.5

During a remarkably busy Monday morning, Audrey, the nursery's full-time finance administrator, takes a call, listens for a moment and then drops the phone, screams and faints. The admin assistant calls for the first aider and Audrey is looked after on the office floor. The nursery manager, Lisa, rushes in, asks what has happened and picks up the phone, asking what is going on. She too, drops onto a chair. Audrey's daughter Amy has called to say that Scott, her brother and Audrey's 17-year-old son, has been involved in a road traffic accident whilst on his bike in town; he's been taken away in an ambulance 'but it isn't looking too good…'

What happened next?

Audrey was revived; she phoned her husband and arranged to meet him at the hospital. A taxi was called and cash was given from the petty cash box; Audrey wanted to go on her own. Later that evening the manager received the sad news that Scott had died on the operating table. What next?

Lisa called Audrey and told her to take as much time as she needed. The staff team were told the news as they came into work, but most already knew through the staff WhatsApp group. Lisa called those who were not on the rota for that day.

One pressing concern was that no one, not even the manager, knew how to complete the invoicing tasks that Audrey was part way through when she left the previous day. Lisa was then preoccupied for days whilst they sorted out the invoicing system and set about the numerous outstanding tasks, now without the skill and expertise of an experienced financial admin worker.

Scott had attended the nursery and was known personally to the three older and long-standing staff members. They were rallying around Audrey at home and were tired, distracted and preoccupied at work. Three weeks later, because so many of the staff wanted to attend the funeral, the nursery closed for the afternoon. Parents had been told by the staff what had happened to Audrey's family. Some wrote letters and cards which were passed on to her. Some of the children noticed Audrey was not in the office, a favourite place for them to linger on their way to the lunch queue.

The manager asked the part-time admin worker to increase their hours to assist with Audrey's work. After four weeks absence from work, Lisa approached Audrey to ascertain if and when she might be ready to return to work. Audrey said she was ready and came back the following Monday.

All the staff greeted Audrey warmly and she settled at her desk. She sat and stared into space for half an hour. The manager asked her if she was ok, she said she was, and the manager suggested she could turn on the computer and check the diary? After a few failed attempts to log in to the computer, Audrey left to take a toilet break. After 20 minutes she had not returned so Lisa sent someone to check on her. Audrey was found sobbing in a cubicle, claiming she was 'useless and can't do it'. This pattern of arriving at the nursery, getting upset and doing no work, and then going home late morning continued all week.

The manager called Audrey at home at the end of the week and asked if she wanted more time off. Audrey said she wanted to get back to normal and came back in on the Monday. She was tearful, jumpy, forgetful and struggled to complete tasks that, pre-bereavement, would take her around 30 minutes. Some of her work was slapdash, she was absent minded and could not follow instructions, and became snappy when asked questions.

It was obvious to everyone that Audrey was struggling, and a solution needed to be found. The children who no longer got to chat with her in the doorway asked where she was.

Work in the nursery office reached a critical stage when Lisa once again had to revisit the invoicing system abandoned by Audrey. It quickly became apparent that many parents had not been invoiced and owed several weeks' fees, with some arrears amounting to more than £1,000. This was embarrassing, inefficient, confusing and showed the nursery in a bad light; allowing families to run up debts ran contrary to their policy and was not good practice. The part-time admin assistant was trained to do all the invoicing and cash-flow forecast; thus, that issue was dealt with satisfactorily.

The manager visited Audrey at her home whilst her husband was there. Audrey said she was embarrassed by her 'failures at work'. Lisa gently explained that she was not a failure, she was grief stricken and maybe more time away from work would be for the best. Her husband gently suggested that she needed proper time to grieve and not be distracted by going to work.

Ways forward

Audrey took unpaid leave from work for 12 months. She had a phased return to work with hours and days to suit her. She decreased her hours and settled into a rhythm of work that gave her plenty of time to rest at home and not get overwhelmed by the pressured office environment around finances, most of it requiring adherence to strict deadlines. Her colleague continued in the finance admin role and their roles were swapped.

Lisa found out about a local group for parents who were coping with the death of a child. Initially hesitant about attending, Audrey found the meetings helpful, supportive and eventually looked forward to meeting up regularly with likeminded parents.

Whilst most of the staff were sympathetic, after a few weeks of tears and upset from Audrey, there was some muttering that 'she should be over it by now'. Lisa used team meetings and supervision to discuss this, asking the staff what they thought should happen.

Reflective points for further action

For the child

- Audrey's colleagues were distracted when Scott died, and this would have been apparent to the children in their care. So, whilst the death was one step removed from life in the nursery, and the children and their families in it, it still affected them.
- If the children asked where Audrey was (as she was not in her office), they could have been told she was not working that day and that would probably have been an adequate explanation.

For the adult

- Give staff time to talk through the circumstances. What would they like to do for Audrey?
- Do not take reliable, hardworking and efficient staff for granted! Ensure that crucial administrative tasks are understood by other workers in the team and that you are not reliant on the expertise of one specific employee.

- The same can be applied to nursery staff who undertake particular roles, like equalities representatives, special educational needs coordinators and keyworkers for particular children. All work in the nursery should have a proper job description, and all workers should have an 'understudy'. This will ensure that the smooth running of the nursery continues. Even if key staff are absent, the children and their families should suffer as little disruption as possible if there is a change in personnel.

- Allow scheduled time for staff to shadow each other so they can learn and understand their colleague's duties and key skills. This can be part of everyone's personal development plan and annual appraisal.

- It was helpful for parents to be told what had happened to Scott. The nursery is a close 'family', a community in its own right, and it is important to be transparent if the staff appear below par, or as happened with the non-issuance of invoices, there was a reason for a lack of professionalism.

- Were all the staff supported through the initial and ongoing period of upset after Scott's death? Three had known him since babyhood, and they in turn took time and care to support Audrey. Who supported them?

- As previously explained, bereavement and grief are not something to tidy away or 'get over'. There is no time limit to feeling and living through grief.

- Speak about Scott. This would not upset Audrey because she was already thinking about him. It is just a kind reminder that you care and that you are thinking of him too.

Case study 5.6

Barbara was an experienced and well-liked childminder. She contacted us in a state of great upset. The parents of a four-year-old girl in her care had telephoned to say that her infant brother had died in hospital following a life-limiting illness he had had since his birth two months earlier. Barbara was shocked and upset for the family and for the girl.

However, she was very troubled and in turmoil because she was a committed Christian and the family were Hindus. She could not accept their differing religious stances regarding death and the afterlife and was so conflicted she felt she no longer wanted anything to do with the family.

What happened next?

Barbara was a good, kind and sensitive person. It was important to support her as she was so troubled by the circumstances she found herself in. We helped her under-stand and acknowledge the ongoing needs of the little girl in her care and the grief of her parents, and separate this practical need for kind, compassionate, ongoing care from the conflicted feelings that she had about a religious faith different to her own. Barbara was in a unique position as the childminder: already known to and trusted by the family, she was familiar with their needs and routines. It would have been very difficult for the parents if she had withdrawn, and bewildering and even more upsetting for the little girl.

There had to be a post-mortem and a lengthy investigation with the hospital, which meant that the funeral – usually a cremation within 24 hours of death within the Hindu faith – was delayed by many weeks. Barbara also told the other families for whom she worked what had happened. She did this with the permission of the bereaved family.

Ways forward

I supported Barbara to continue to childmind the little girl during that period. The continuity of care given by Barbara helped this four-year-old get through a very difficult family time. Her parents were distraught, distracted and unable to meet her needs in any meaningful way. I gave Barbara contact details to pass on to the parents for support through the children's hospital.

I urged Barbara to talk to her priest and her bible study group to help her deal with her feelings of anxiety and conflict about the differences in faith. I spoke to Barbara weekly to help her cope with the great sadness she felt about the death of the baby and her sorrow about the grief of the girl and her parents. She borrowed books about death and dying to use with the children in her care. She also read about the Hindu faith and shared her findings with her church group.

After a few weeks, the funeral was arranged. Barbara decided she could, and would, attend; she took care of the girl and helped her during the cremation so her parents could support each other during the service.

Soon after, the family returned to India because they felt they needed the support of their family to help them through their grief. They wrote Barbara a wonderful, heartfelt 'thank you' letter. They were grateful for her support during their darkest time, her thoughtful care for their little daughter when they could not deal with her, and her kindness in attending the funeral and supporting them and explaining the situation to the other parents.

Reflective points for further action

For the child

- Continuity of care was very important. The child was familiar with Barbara, and happy with the rhythm and routine of the day-to-day with her.
- Barbara rose to the challenge and excelled at giving this bereaved family her undivided attention, thus helping them through a dreadful few weeks.
- The child felt safe with her and trusted her.

For the adult

- It is important that the faith (or no faith) of the bereaved family is respected and that whatever the family ask that the child be told is adhered to.
- Belief in different things is a good conversation starter with children when discussing death: e.g. 'My Nana's in heaven!' 'Well, what's that?' 'It's in the sky and my Nana is with her Nana and everyone eats ice cream and they have kittens and they're happy.' 'What do the rest of you think about that?'
- Childminders often work at home and without colleagues. They are especially vulnerable when dealing with a significant family crisis or periods of change because they do not have a staff team around them to share the load or to talk things through as they happen.

Key ideas from this chapter

- Be respectful regarding what the family has already told the child and *do not* deviate towards your own personal beliefs.
- Keep contact lists up-to-date for families and colleagues, and keep passwords, etc., safe but accessible.
- Consider what to include in your setting's bereavement policy and what procedures are important. Revisit it regularly with your staff team.
- There is never an ideal time, but encourage staff to discuss how they would talk to children about death and dying.
- Buy some good books for children and adults about bereavement. Read them together and practice what to say to children and their adults (see the book list in Appendix A).
- Contact charities and online support as needed.

- Contact your local authority early years team to use as a sounding board, or for additional resources and support if needed.

- Support the supporters.

- Keep an up-to-date list of local grief counsellors and give the details to families and staff as need. The local authority early years team may be able to assist in finding the appropriate support.

- Allow staff time to attend support sessions if necessary.

- A staff team that has considered their personal and the setting's response to a death affecting a child in their care will be more confident and better able to look after the child, the family and each other.

- One in ten employees are affected by a bereavement at any given time.

- A workplace has a duty of care to all of the children in their care and their adults, and to the workers in their employ.

- If you are a lone worker or supporting one, meet or speak to them regularly. It can be lonely and isolating working alone. Use support networks, childminder groups and early years professionals for guidance and help with difficult issues.

- Ensure you are up to date regarding employees' rights about compassionate and parental leave, and ensure that staff contracts are up to date. Check out the UK government's Statutory Parental Bereavement Pay and Leave: Employer Guide at www.gov.uk/employers-parental-bereavement-pay-leave.

- As an employee you're allowed time off work to deal with an emergency involving a dependant. A dependant could be a spouse, partner, child, grandchild, parent or someone else who depends on you for care. You are allowed a reasonable amount of time off to deal with the emergency, but there is no set amount of time as it depends on the specific situation. There are no limits on how many times you can take time off for dependents. Your employer may want to talk to you if they think time off is affecting your work.

- Check your information-sharing policies and protocols. WhatsApp messaging is easy, quick, and convenient, but who is receiving the messages? Be careful about imparting confidential, sensitive, personal information in an informal way.

- See Chapter 4 for additional ideas.

Reference

Dyregrov, A. (2008) *Grief in Young Children: A Handbook for Adults*. London: Jessica Kingsley.

6 Resources and settings

Staff

The most valuable, most important and most precious resources in any care and education setting is the staff team.

Practical resources such as books, toys and so on are helpful but mean little without good, kind and thoughtful practitioners using them effectively as tools to help the children feel better and deal with new and difficult feelings and changes in their lives. Practitioners will already know the child who is bereaved or suffering loss, and their family, and some, like the child's key worker, will understand their personality very well. Key workers will be well known and trusted by the child and their family; they already have a relationship with each other and will be familiar with the different means of expression the child uses. Yet, most nursery settings are a cohesive community in their own right, and the backbone to this 'family' functioning efficiently is a well-organised, enthusiastic and hardworking staff team.

Keeping everyone informed, up-to-date and aware of the facts is key here. Be thoughtful; get the balance right by not encouraging speculation and gossip whilst still following your information-sharing protocols and not divulging confidential and private details inappropriately.

Staff members can hold children and give hugs; they can sing gentle, crooning songs that settle and comfort upset children. Practitioners can empathise with the adult's anguish and pain but rise above it to really care for and help their child. Because of this it is important that staff members should be cared for too. They should be well equipped, well trained, well supported, and supervised efficiently and often. Without good, skilled, experienced practitioners there is a danger that even the most well-equipped nursery will not be able to provide the best care and education for children. This is a fundamental point. Staff are thus the best and most valuable resource in any early years care and education setting and should be respected, nurtured and valued.

An important point underpinning this grief and loss work is that the staff need to get good communication 'right': this is of paramount importance between the staff team itself and then between the staff and families. It is important to remember that, when thinking about communication, the whole team should be included. This includes cleaners, mealtime assistants, cooks, drivers, caretakers, volunteers, students on placement, visiting professionals, gardeners – in fact, anyone who will potentially have contact with the child and their family. The amount of information shared should of course be appropriate to the role undertaken. A child will seek comfort and support from anyone they feel safe with, and this may not always be the most obvious person or their key worker.

Training

Individual staff members will feel more confident and find it easier to talk with the adults and children who are bereaved and/or suffering loss if they have had some good-quality training. Many settings have had their training budgets cut and feel that it is beyond their capacity to access professional training. In Appendix C we include some ideas for training, and there are other ways to access expertise. The manager of the setting might contact the early years team in the local authority. They may have an experienced worker who might be able to come in for an informal lunchtime talk with the staff team or attend an after-hours staff meeting. The team might offer free or low-cost bereavement training.

If there is no time or budget for training, there is a waiting list or there is nothing on offer, there might be local charities that run courses or give bereavement support who could phone and talk it through with the manager, who could then cascade the information down to all staff.

Crisis situations

Ideally, we recommend this training as a care element of the setting's practice. However, we also recognise that this is not always the case and that it might occur in the middle of a difficult situation, like the scenarios that we described in Chapters 4 and 5. The best way to address the staff team's needs in this case is to give workers time to talk through the current situation. This enables them to become familiar with their own feelings and, importantly, with what will happen in the setting with the family. Make sure everyone knows the daily session plan for the room or key worker looking after the child. It is imperative that everyone knows what the child has been told at home about the change in their circumstances and that, irrespective of individual points of views or beliefs, they are consistent with this as discussed with the parents (see Chapter 5).

Managers of settings may already have workers who are experienced and can offer advice and support to less-experienced colleagues. I recall a young woman on an early years bereavement training course who at the age of 22 had coped with the deaths of a younger sibling, her mum and her dad, and was helping to look after her terminally ill Grandma. This did not make her a 'death' expert, but her calm, honest and practical responses to the questions and scenarios posed were a lesson to us all.

As mentioned, there is no right time in a busy setting's year to book a trainer or send someone on a seminar. It is easy to put it off because it does not seem relevant to your present circumstances. But, we would ask, what about tomorrow, next term, the year after? Workers who have had time to read the range of books that are on offer for the children, and books for personal development if they are particularly interested, will respond better to the upset around a bereaved child. Their knowledge and understanding will have grown, and they will have developed enough confidence to speak to the child and their carers.

Child Bereavement UK have an excellent website full of useful information, but by far their best resources are their series of short guidance films (see www.childbereavementuk.org/). These films, each between 2 and 5 minutes long, take a whole range of real-life situations and give instant advice on how to respond and what to say to a child. Topics range from how to tell a child about death to explaining a still-birth or miscarriage, as well as many more potential scenarios. Beautifully written, well presented and very easy to follow, these simple scripts are extremely well done. If you have been put on the spot with no time to seek advice or guidance elsewhere, visit this website. They also have a telephone helpline (0800 02 888 40). Use the short films as training tools in the workplace and encourage your staff team to watch as many as possible.

Winston's Wish is another wonderful charity that provides sample policies, letters and lots of online help (see www.winstonswish.org/). Their training courses are excellent. You can call their free helpline on 0800 020021 for therapeutic advice on supporting a grieving child or young person following the death of a loved one.

Supervision and support of staff in crisis

Staff need guidance and support, and one management strategy is to do this through robust and regular supervision. This is the formal aspect of checking in with the worker to ensure that they have the tools, skills and necessary knowledge to undertake their duties safely and without undue stress. If you feel that you need to improve your supervision methods, we would suggest:

- Asking trusted colleagues in other settings.
- Using their template/plan.
- Going back to the local authority: they will have resources to help; alternatively, there are some good supervision templates online that are free to use.

If the staff member under supervision is very upset and anxious we would suggest.

- Enabling them to have some time out.
- Perhaps instigating a job-share situation, at least temporarily.
- Agreeing that they can take longer breaks to help them to cope.

Some staff who are anxious about working with a bereaved child will shy away from being in the room with them, perhaps even shirking their responsibilities. This can be awkward and cause some resentment amongst the team if it is not dealt with. Either in supervision or during a quiet interlude away from the team, you could ask them why this is happening and explain what is expected of them. They may not realise that everyone feels nervous about taking on an extremely upset or withdrawn child if they have not done it before. They may be dealing with their own grief or unresolved issues following a death you may know nothing about. Only by gentle questioning can someone's real feelings be revealed.

Practitioners may find it hard to take care of the child's needs unless they have a grip on their own responses and feelings. This is similar to what the parents are experiencing. Some workers shy away from the bereaved child and their family because they are frightened of the strength of their own feelings and of crying in front of them. It is not a weakness to show your own emotions, and it can help the family and the child to express their feelings. It is not just children who grow and learn from sharing feelings, experiences and offering each other support and understanding. To respond to the needs of others, childcare workers must first be aware of their own feelings and how they respond in various circumstances.

Allow staff to take some time out if they become overly upset or find the circumstances draining. Check if they would benefit from external counselling and investigate what is on offer locally. Source recommendations from trusted colleagues in other settings or, once again, approach the local authority early years team for advice.

Anyone working with a bereaved family will need some or all of the help listed above to do this work well. In our experience, some staff feel they have to perform at a very high level, and that to ask for help or show their own vulnerability is a weakness and will result in their being judged as lacking. Make sure that each member of staff can talk freely and confidentially in the safe space of the office or the staff room so they can be truthful and talk through their feelings, impressions and reactions. As mentioned earlier, it is extremely exhausting dealing with death, loss and crisis situations all day. There needs to be some self-care and lighter moments in order to provide relief.

A good supply of fresh water, tea/coffee, snacks and treats in a quiet space is the ideal. We know this is not always possible; we know that some nurseries do not have staff rooms. But try to find a quiet space for two chairs away from the rest of the session so workers can chat quietly, cry, hug each other and read through the next session plan so they feel refreshed and prepared.

Policies and procedures

Once you have staff that are capable and confident, they will need a source of reference and back-up for the policies and procedures you have in place. Again, Child Bereavement UK (www.childbereavementuk.org/) provides a sample policy/charter. This is written primarily for school-age children, but it is a good crib sheet to start you thinking and most of it is relevant to an early years setting. If it is not appropriate to ask very young child certain questions, you will need to ask their parents instead. There are two sections: 1) the death of a child or member of staff; and 2) supporting a bereaved child. It is particularly good in terms of listing staff roles, responsibilities and procedures. If you are short of time and the situation is urgent, start there and go back to the ethos and objectives later. There are templates for letters to parents, too.

The following is a simple nursery policy that we have written. It gets to the point but does not itemise the procedures. In our opinion, this is a useful starting point to take to the staff team and talk it through, so that it can be made relevant to each setting that uses it.

> We aim to support all children and their families throughout their time in nursery and especially at times of bereavement when a family member, friend or loved one, including the family pet, dies.

When adults are dealing with the shock of a bereavement and coping with their own grief, it is a very difficult time for families. It is additional pressure to meet the needs of a very young child who may not understand about death but is aware that their adults are upset and distracted.

We will adapt the following procedures to suit the child's ongoing needs:

- We ask that the family inform the nursery of the death as soon as they are able and decide with the staff who should be told, and in what detail, about the change in the child's circumstances.

- We will meet the parents/carers without the child present, away from the setting if needed, or speak by phone, to ascertain what the child has been told about the death and what the family want the practitioners to say to the child. We will discuss and agree any necessary extra support needed at this initial stage.

- We recognise that sending the child to nursery at this time will maintain the child's regular routine, which will be helpful, but the child may be tired, distracted or not feel like participating very much. We will ensure that there is time and space for them to eat and rest as needed.

- We will support the child's key worker and understand that there may be a change in the child's behaviour, and we will adapt staffing arrangements and the child's day to make this as stress free as we are able to.

- Parents/carers will have direct contact with the key worker, or, in their absence, the manager.

- We will be flexible wherever possible to adapt the sessions and the content of the curriculum as needed by the child and their family.

- We will feedback to the parents/carers anything relevant or important that happens during the child's day at nursery and will discuss with them ways forward as time passes.

- We will review this policy annually and amend the procedures as needed for each bereavement in nursery.

Make your policy relevant to your staff and setting. Revisit it at least annually and revise it once you have used it. Your real-time experiences will be a valuable resource here. You might take some time to think about past crisis situations that have been dealt with. What worked well? What can you change now you have all had recent experience of bereavement in the nursery? Who is new and needs 'inset' time to read the policy and help to understand the thinking behind these procedures?

Curriculum activities

Young children do not necessarily have the language skills to express how they feel – they show us what they want and the emotions with which they are dealing through their behaviour. To enable this, the setting needs to examine its curriculum and source activities that will support the child's exploration of their feelings and memories of grief and loss in a nurturing, safe and inclusive play environment. Young children can struggle with grief due to their level of cognitive development and their ability to understand and manage emotions, and may re-enact the traumatic event through symbolic play and movement. And all children need to play as a way of exploring and learning from their environment.

Whether it is one-to-one play with a trusted adult, lone play or a group play session, the child will need to 'tell the story' of what has happened. This will aid their knowledge and understanding of recent events and will give them the opportunity to ask questions, listen to answers from trusted adults and perhaps play amongst their peers, who may also have questions – and maybe some answers. Staff should observe the child's play because it will be very revealing about what they understand and how they are feeling, even if they cannot articulate all of those feelings.

Puppets, teddies and dolls

Using toys – in particular puppets, teddies and dolls – facilitates the child's self-expression. While they play, observe them to see if they pretend that the puppet is them. They might shout at it 'Grandad's dead!' over and over. They might tell the doll about being put in the ground. They might ask the teddy if they have been to heaven. These examples show that in acting out that their toy dog is feeling sad, for example, the child is processing their feelings without confronting the loss directly, and this protects them from being overwhelmed by their emotions.

> Children can use puppets to act out secrets or hidden feelings without identifying these thoughts and feelings as being their own. Having the children perform puppet work behind a barrier allows them to feel they are hidden and safe when they speak.
>
> (Goldman, 2001, p. 112)

Whatever the child plays, whatever resources they use, it is an excellent way for them to get rid of their aggression, calm and comfort themselves, deal with their anxiety and try to find answers. Unless asked a direct question it is better to leave the child to explore all of this through play. They may want to talk about this play afterwards – or not.

Small world play

Small world play is crucial in enabling the child to use their own experiences of the world to build on their imaginative skills. In this play the child acts out these experiences in a controlled way, and it also allows them to experiment with fantasy play and incorporate their own ideas. Scenarios can often change or be adapted, enabling the child to think of new ideas or ways to extend the play.

Having play materials such as doctor and nurse sets with bandages, syringes, thermometers, etc., is very helpful to a child who is trying to express their feelings through actions instead of words. Acting out being the doctor can help them choose different roles and different endings; they may like to be the doctor who can help sick people, so that they do not die, and are instead saved: 'Why didn't the doctor give him more medicine?'; 'Will we get ill and die?'

They might act out driving the ambulance to collect Grandad and take him to the hospital. Acting this scenario out can lead the child to display a range of emotions and use their problem-solving skills to try to fix the problem and continue the play successfully: 'Grandad is in hospital. Oh no! He's died!' Children will often learn a great deal about cause and effect through their small world play as they have a great deal of control over the direction of events. This allows them to experiment with different actions, leading them to understand different outcomes: 'Grandad's in hospital. The doctor mended him.' 'Oh no, he's dead now!' 'Now he's going to burn! [i.e. cremation]!'

Children might find relief in playing out fantasies of revenge or punishment. It may look disturbing to the adults around them, but it helps them process what has happened. Also, it could lessen their feelings of helplessness by giving them control over the play and the scenario that they have set up. To onlookers, some of the actions and comments may seem gruesome and bear no relation to reality. However, the child is acting out what they think and feel, which is altogether healthier than not getting it out into the open. Children will always fill in any blanks in what they have been told and in their knowledge and understanding of the facts with their own fantasies and misunderstandings.

Feelings resources

There are many resources you can use to help children express their feelings. Together, you could look at 'feelings cards' and posters where a child's face is drawn or photographed to show a particular expression or a feeling, in order to open up discussion: 'Oh look, this little girl is crying. I wonder why? What do you think has happened?' The child will respond (or not!). You might follow up with 'How did you feel when Grandad died? What can you tell me about that?' Makaton cards are useful for this type of question and answer, too.

Books

Using books as 'door openers' on difficult topics like death and bereavement, moving house, losing teddy, changing schools, etc., is doubly useful. First, the child will realise that other people have experienced the same things they are going through. Second, it allows the child time to reflect on what has happened and ask questions: 'That's how I'm feeling too!' See Appendix A.

Drawing and painting

Art activity – creative expression, drawing and especially painting, getting messy – is a great outlet for pent-up feelings that for the child do not seem to have anywhere to go. An example of this could be making a mask. The practitioner might ask the child who the mask is. It might be someone they miss or something quite different. Children's play is frequently repetitive, and the same questions may be asked over and over again. It is good for the practitioner to encourage drawing or painting of the child's feelings or more factual portrayals of who the dead or lost person was and their relationship to the child: 'This is a picture on the beach. I am eating my crisps. This is Nana and Dad and Mum is there but she's dead now.' 'Was it a very special day? What did you enjoy the most?' 'Mum's in heaven now' 'Oh, what do you think that's like?' These are examples of open-ended questions that can lead to discussion.

Children gouging out thick black marks in sticky, messy paint can seem aggressive, and early years workers have told us they find it quite alarming. But, we ask, how else can a child 'exorcise' their deep, frightened and angry feelings about their father's death or leaving their home when they do not have the emotional literacy or the vocabulary to say how sad and upset they are? They are missing their Dad and as yet have no understanding that it is permanent or, in the case of a separation, that things will be different hereafter. The adults in their life are sad, taking little notice of them and crying all the time, and nothing is like it was before.

Playdough and cornflour

Some children do not like playing with cornflour mixed with water (gloop), but for those who do it is good practice to encourage them to spend as long as they like, poking, smoothing, sliding, pinching and stroking the gloop. Pummelling and smacking playdough is another sensory experience that is a great outlet for their feelings, particularly if they are feeling anxious and have no words left.

Sand and water play

Sand and water come into their own with an upset child. These nursery basics are simple yet effective, and the child usually needs little encouragement to engage with them, so the play can form part of their coping strategies. Pouring, tipping, filling and emptying can be accompanied by a narrative of recent events in their lives.

Physical play

Physical play – such as climbing, running, skipping, throwing balls, spinning hoops, waving scarves and hiding under blankets – forms the cornerstone of good practice in a setting's day. It also takes on additional emphasis when the child doing the play is over-wrought, crying, smiling, chattering, sharing, not sharing and dealing with their grief. Children need to use their bodies, exercise, chase their friends, expel energy, curl up in a den and be in charge in the home corner. Children will put aside their grief and 'big feelings' for the sheer fun and enjoyment of playing. This respite is natural and does not mean they have 'got over it'.

Remembrance

Nursery and the familiar people in it have a special place in the child's life and can be especially important in supporting the child when they are remembering their dead relative or pet. Not strictly a play category, remembrance is a catch-all term for activities with the child, or groups of children, to make cards or pictures for themselves to show their family or to make playdough people that represent the person held dear.

It is helpful to do this one-to-one with the grieving child to start with, and then together with their peer group. Children can talk about their feelings in a small circle or group and ask questions of the bereaved child. It is often surprising how direct and matter-of-fact young children can be. The adults around them might be embarrassed or upset by their blunt questions or comments to each other. This does not mean that the children do not have feelings; rather, it means that they are not bound by the unspoken rules of societal behaviour in the same way that the adults around them are.

Winston's Wish (see www.winstonswish.org) has many lovely suggestions to help make memory jars and memory boxes, which are a personal collection of precious items that mean something to the child and that are put into a container to keep safe. They are looked at and talked about as often as needed. This is also an extremely helpful activity to do when the whole setting is involved, such as after the death of a staff member or child. Memory jars can sit on the side, and as time goes by they are a gentle reminder to everyone that this is the new reality for the bereaved child/children. The grieving child may ask to handle the jar on anniversaries and at times of stress or sadness, but may also proudly show their peers what they have in the jar and tell them why they have the keepsakes.

Having a photo in their lunch box, rucksack or pocket can be a real comfort for some children. Others will see it and it can spark some interesting conversations. An observing adult might find some valuable material that will help them support that child. It might be useful to hear how other children respond to the child and any questions that they might ask. As a result of this observation, the practitioner could gauge that the time is right to read one of the books about grief and loss again at circle time to help children who wish to articulate their feelings. It might also be a way of ascertaining what knowledge and understanding the children have about death. Afterwards, the practitioner could make some notes and feed this information back to the rest of the staff team.

Persona Dolls

Persona Dolls are one of the best resources for the setting at all times, but they are invaluable during bereavement (see https://personadoll.uk/the-persona-doll-approach).

With thoughtful and careful use of a Persona Doll in the setting, children's communication and listening skills are developed: 'Persona Doll stories encourage empathy, critical thinking and problem solving' (www.personadolluk.org). These very special dolls are not toys and are kept away from the children when not being used in a session. They are big, soft bodied dolls, dressed in children's clothes, and are large enough to sit on the worker's lap and for children to hug. Each doll is handmade and is unique. Some are chosen because they look like the majority of the children in the setting, others are chosen because they portray a 'difference' not represented in the nursery. Once the backstory has been written and the stories unfold with the circle-time sessions, you have a very powerful tool to use.

The crucial difference is that each doll is given a persona, a backstory, by the setting/practitioner. Once this has been devised, it is written in the doll's journal and does not change. Every time the doll 'visits' nursery, the purpose of the visit is written up, so the story continues and stays the same.

The children know they are dolls but treat them as friends.

Through the doll's story and regular visits to circle time, children are encouraged to listen, empathise and come up with solutions. Persona Dolls can also go on trips with the children so when they next have circle time, they feed back if the doll enjoyed themselves or was worried and so on. When used in an environment in which a range of life styles, traditions and cultures are appreciated, carefully chosen Persona Dolls and their stories encourage children to value and respect not only various skin colours, but also a range of hair textures and facial features. Introducing Dolls that do not reflect the children in the group can promote cross-cultural respect and understanding. This is particularly important where the children are all from the same ethnic or cultural group and are monolingual.

(www.personadolluk.org)

Whilst the initial and ongoing purpose of Persona Dolls was to encourage and develop equalities in settings, the usefulness at particular times in a nursery's experience can be immeasurable, especially during grief and bereavement. It is especially helpful when the bereaved child is already a member of a cultural minority and the doll reflects part or all of their culture.

Children's emotional involvement in the stories is crucial. It helps to capture and deepen their interest, arouses their curiosity and challenges them intellectually. In their everyday speaking voice, practitioners tell the children what the Dolls have come to 'tell' them about. They encourage children to think critically and outside the box, praise the ability of those who speak more than one language, boost self-esteem and confidence and, crucially, give everyone time to reflect and respond.

If your setting is unfamiliar with Persona Dolls and the concept around their use, you are missing out on a fantastic and empowering resource that delights both children and practitioners. Go to the website and watch the videos. The doll will be helpful in assisting with many issues beyond the current bereavement.

Case study 6.1

Ferdinand, our Persona Doll, is visiting the small group of children all sitting on the floor. Ferdinand is sitting on the practitioner's lap with his head turned to her shoulder. The practitioner greets the children and says that she is pleased that Ferdinand has come to visit them today.

Before she can continue, two children start the conversation:

'Why is he hiding?' 'What's the matter Ferdi?' 'I want to see his face!'

The practitioner leans to Ferdinand and asks him if there is something the matter. Ferdinand 'replies' in her ear. 'Ferdinand is sad today.'

'Why?' 'What's wrong Ferdi?'

'Ferdinand is sad because his cat has died.'

Ferdinand turns slowly to the group but puts his head down, looking at his lap.

'Is he crying?' 'What happened to the cat?' 'Where is the cat? I want to see it!' Laughter and squeals from the group.

The practitioner leans in to listen to Ferdinand. 'He says that his cat was very old and died in the garden under the rose bush'.

'Did Ferdi see it?' 'What's dead mean?' 'My hamster died at Christmas!'
A child gets up and holds Ferdinand's hand.

'Ferdinand's Mum found Pusskin in the garden. Pusskin was an old, old cat. Her body stopped working, her heart stopped beating, her brain stopped thinking and her body died.'

'My Grandpa died!' 'Will my cat die?' There is chatter amongst the children.

Ferdinand looks up at the children and around the circle.

The children say 'Hey Ferdi, over here!' 'I'm sad about your cat!' 'Did you cry?'

The practitioner asks the children: 'What can you do because Ferdi is sad? 'How can we help him feel better?'

'I can hug him!' 'He can have my raisins' 'Tell us about your cat' 'We can make him a love card to take home' 'I can draw cats'.

The practitioner asks Ferdinand what he thinks about the children's nice suggestions. He answers in her ear: 'Ferdinand says that he is already feeling better because you are being so kind to him.' The children take turns to stroke Ferdinand's hair and hug him. He is taken into the children's circle and sits on their laps in turn.

The practitioner lets the children talk feely to Ferdinand, observing how some of the children answer for him. When circle time ends, the practitioner retrieves the doll and the children sing goodbye to Ferdinand, who waves and blows kisses to them and then is taken from the room by the practitioner.

The children move to the arts and crafts area and draw pictures of cats (including dead cats) and Ferdinand. These are put into the special scrapbook kept for drawings and photos of the doll's visits to the nursery, which is freely available for everyone to look at at any time.

Reflective point

It may have been appropriate amongst the clamouring at Ferdinand to answer the question 'Will my cat die?' The practitioner must judge whether it is more important to stay in the moment and go with the flow of chat and questions or break the flow and address a specific query. Provided you do go back to it, you can answer those questions later, after the Persona Doll session. This would be a good time to use the books and stories about life cycles and living and dying at circle time. See Chapters 4 and 5 for further information. Flag up with colleagues what you are doing.

Using the Persona Doll on this occasion would have been supportive of a child in the session who was already dealing with bereavement, without drawing particular attention to them. It would show them that it happens to other people too and they are not alone, as well as demonstrating that their peers can be kind. Maybe they will gain the confidence to speak out about their situation, their feelings. It also allows the practitioner to speak to them later about Ferdinand: 'Ferdinand was sad because his cat died. Is that how you feel about Nanna?'

Key ideas from this chapter

- The best resource in an early years setting are the staff team.
- The staff need to be encouraged and nurtured.
- Training in grief and loss is very useful. It can be accessed through Appendix C in this book, online, via informal chats with colleagues or the local support team, or by using books.
- Use staff meetings to discuss the current and ongoing situation. What is next? Who is going to be responsible for it?
- Supervision is the key to settled and well-performing staff.
- Policies and procedures are an underpinning toolkit. They need to be revisited annually. Use your experience to update them, show the staff team, make sure they read them and answer any questions and take on board their suggestions to improve, add to or change them.
- Curriculum activities and daily planning are essential. What can you offer all the children and the bereaved child to help them express their feelings? What are they expressing as they play with the clay, the playdough?
- As they play, nursery staples such as sand, water, playdough and rice are helpful. Do not fuss about the clearing up, the children will help. What is the current favourite? What new words do they have? 'I like pouring the water on my feet. It makes them wriggle and I feel happy!'
- Frequent outdoor play, even if it's just mooching around the garden, is essential to 'break the spell' for a child having a sad and difficult day. Let's get the endorphins working!
- Be proactive in enabling children to make love cards, memory boxes or jars. Give them the time and space to make them and talk about why they matter to them. Explain in advance to their parents and carers what they are making and why. If the

parents are anxious about subsequently having to talk to their child (again) about the death, explain to them how important it is for them to speak to their child about what has happened in a natural and gentle way. This can be hard as they may want to avoid more tears (both theirs and the child's) and may not want to deal with any more upset.

Reference

Goldman, L. (2001) *Breaking the Silence*. London: Routledge.

7 | Crises and disasters in terms of loss and grief

This chapter uses the current (at the time of writing) COVID-19 pandemic as an overall case study, but the wider theme is that of supporting children in times of crisis. We think that the issues we discuss here could be applied to any of the disasters and crisis situations that adults and children may have been or are currently affected by. This includes natural disasters such as flooding, hurricanes, earthquakes and famine, as well as other crisis situations, such as school shootings, riots and war. We have examined specific support for children who are refugees in a case study in Chapter 4. Many of these situations share the same details of privation: families and individuals being confined to their living quarters (lockdown), a lack of contact with friends and extended family, an outside threat to be protected from, and difficulty in accessing food and other supplies. There is inevitably a disruption to children's (and parents') normal routines and education. These are sad and desperate situations, and we hope that a child's experience of these in their life is limited and ideally non-existent. As carers and parents we need to reflect on how we can prepare for something so far beyond the usual realms of our lives.

The current bad stuff

As I am writing this (May 2020) the UK, Europe and the wider world are in the middle of a pandemic due to the COVID-19 virus. I am in lockdown in my flat, and my usual routines and habits are in complete disarray. I am able to venture out once a day for a walk and can only see my family and friends virtually. All of my social groups have moved online and we are having to get to grips with Skype, Houseparty and Zoom. Virtual entertainment is now more important to me than ever before, and I'm pleased that I am able to access Amazon and Netflix.

An adapted version of this chapter, 'Coronavirus: Responding to Children's Feelings of Loss and Fear', was published online by *Nursery World* on 18 June 2020.

Most of my world has been turned upside down and I feel like I'm living in a bad dream. I don't know how long this will go on for or what the world will look like when it is over. It has made me think about children and how they are coping with the loss of their routines and usual way of life. They could be missing their usual contact with friends, family, daycare and school. They will also be sensing the stress of the adults around them. Children will be overhearing adult talk and absorbing information from the media. Linda Goldman makes this strong and thought-provoking statement:

> The automatic assumption of most adults is that our children are basically happy and carefree. The reality is that the majority of the world's children are grieving children. So many of our boys and girls are born into grief and loss issues that live inside their homes and lay waiting for them outside their doorsteps, on their streets, in their schoolyards, in their classrooms, and around their community. Increasingly, children are traumatised by prevailing social, societal, and natural loss issues in their families, their schools, their nation and their world. Children in the twenty first century live with challenges that were unimaginable for their parents and teachers. Death related tragedies associated with natural disasters, accidents, suicide, homicide and war and non death related traumas such as abandonment and lack of protection, dislocation and loss of property, foster care, hopelessness, bullying, terrorism and abuse and violence.
>
> (Goldman, 2001, p. 182)

In this section I provide no answers, just observations and thoughts. It maybe that in time we will be able to look back on this pandemic and ascertain the effect that it had on young children. At the moment, we are in the middle of it and we can only surmise. For some children, as a result of the virus there has been bereavement within their circle of family and friends. We have already spoken at length about how to support children who have experienced bereavement. The only thing to add here is that it is possible that there was no funeral or group gathering to mark the person's death, and that denial of that outlet for grief will affect the adults around the child and, in turn, the child.

We can say that all children will experience some form of loss during this pandemic. Most children are away from school and nursery, and are being cared for and taught at home. If their parents are essential workers, then children might be with an adult that they're not used to, without any settling-in period. Both parents and children may struggle with these new arrangements. Many people will be working at home and having to juggle this with childcare and education. They may have no experience of teaching or delivering information to young children. Even with online help and support from the child's school, this can be a stressful task for parents. It might remind them of their own experiences at school, and these might be very negative indeed. They might try and teach in the way that they were taught, which may be confusing for the child.

With limited access to the outside world, relationships between adults in the household, and with children, can get difficult and tense. This contains elements of a child's nightmare: strife at home and no contact with the outside world.

At one stroke, children have been parted from all that is familiar in their day, be it school or nursery. Many institutions have set up communication with children so that they understand that these significant adults haven't left them, that they are still thinking about them and want to be connected to them. However, the success of this relies on the level of understanding that a child has; this is linked to their age and whether they have any special needs. The future is uncertain and adults cannot deliver the reassurance that children want – they don't know when schools and workplaces will reopen, or when children will be able to see their friends and family again. Children have lost their familiar routines and the established timetables that carry with them known patterns of behaviour. I am aware that some children live in chaotic households where established routines are not the norm; however, for most children there is a pattern of school attendance.

Of course, some children are homeschooled already, and it would be easy to assume that there would be no disruption to their day as their parents and carers are used to the routine of homeschooling. However, these routines might rely on meeting with groups of other children who are homeschooled, visiting museums, playgrounds or other places that are now closed, or travelling to natural beauty spots that they are now unable to access.

For those families without outside space, children may spend much of their day within the same four walls; perhaps they are with younger or older siblings and are having to continually negotiate space and resources in way that they don't usually need to. In the UK we have been able to have one trip outside each day for exercise, but this has not been the case in other European countries, such as Spain, for example, where children have had to remain in their homes.

This will likely be the longest, most sustained period that adults have spent with each other, and perhaps with their children too. The only other similar situation is during family holidays, which is very different from the restrictions that we are currently living under due to the pandemic.

Here, I've spent some time detailing the negative aspects of this situation. I am not doing this in order to be completely hopeless and doom laden, but rather to reflect upon and unpick what children are experiencing at the moment. Of course, everything that they're experiencing the adults are experiencing too. This is overlaid with the more mature and logical understanding that adults have: for example, 'This won't last forever', 'I can take steps to keep myself safe', etc. But inside that adult will be a young child who is frightened, unsure and in need of reassurance.

We have discussed in the book how, as adults, we are used to problem solving and taking care of children. In the current situation, we are limited in terms of how much reassurance we can confidently give. That's a very difficult situation for a parent to be in. The household may seem like a pressure cooker full of unresolved emotions: adults feeling anxious, children feeling anxious, and activities and movements restricted.

There are many vignettes being shared on the Internet at the moment. One that struck me was a man being asked would he like to spend lockdown with A) his wife and children, or B) … and before the interviewer could finish the man said 'B – I choose B!' without knowing what 'B' is! Watching that, I was imagined that many adults, male and female, might be thinking the same thing.

Gender roles might be turned on their head in a household that is in lockdown. Household tasks such as cooking, cleaning and childcare/education will possibly be shared more equally as both parents will be at home – as well as which, there is nowhere for the other parent to remove themselves to. This might be a new situation and can lead to tension and stress. In many households there is just one parent having to cope alone, with no school/nursery, childminder or family members able to offer respite, making life very stressful indeed. Today I read that there are exceptions to the lockdown rule for households where two parents share parenting in different houses, in that children are able to travel from one home to the other. This is a relief to parents who are separated and/or divorced. Some parents will be unable to alternate the care of their children due to enhanced risk of infection; this change may be difficult for a child and they feel the absence of the other parent. The parent who is not seeing the child might feel aggrieved and express this in their online contact, using the child to work through their feelings of anger and disappointment.

In crisis situations small areas of conflict between adults can be magnified; this can add to a child's feelings of loss as they are confined within an arena of adult discord and bewilderment at their lack of control.

Another issue that children might have to deal with is the absence of extended family. On the forums that I have visited there are grandparents talking about missing their grandchildren, and vice versa. Some grandparents are regular carers for grandchildren, taking them to and picking them up from school and nursery, and they will be very much missed in this difficult time.

A short video that I saw showed a woman protesting strongly about being expected to be a teacher to her children: 'Why have you emailed me a music score? I can't read music? What, am I supposed to get my clarinet out?' Luckily there are many support resources available online for children and adults to access – though parents then have the worry that their children are spending even more time glued to a screen.

An additional concern is that while there might be a downturn in street violence as bars and pubs are closed, for those woman and children experiencing domestic abuse the situation will potentially worsen as everyone is confined together for long periods of time and have to depend upon their own resources for activities and entertainment, with little outside support. This is an aspect I discussed with a police liaison worker.

As the period of social avoidance extends, children are missing significant celebrations: for example, their own birthdays and those of family members, in addition to any other celebrations that their family observes. Passover, Eid and Easter all looked very different this year. Children might find it hard to understand why they can't see the people they would usually see and perhaps not get the gifts that they are accustomed to receiving, or having the usual family meals and rituals (attending church, temple or synagogue; visiting family and friends for large gatherings) that they have been part of.

Explaining a crisis situation to children

In the ongoing COVID-19 situation there has been a variety of materials available to support parents in talking about the crisis with their children. I heard one parent referring to the virus as 'glitter' in order to explain how it can spread, and I thought this was a really useful, visual analogy that a child could easily understand. I haven't got a template for what words to use or how to talk to children in a crisis situation. Each child is different, and conversations with them need to be tailored to their age and stage of development. Every parent knows their child best and understands what will make sense to them. I do have some observations to bear in mind when having these conversations, though. As an underpinning point I would say that we cannot shield children from crisis situations, and hence we need to think about the conversations we will have with them and the information they might ask for. Even very young children will notice if the adults around them are upset and anxious and if routines have changed. Older children will be exposed to news and other media, and may well be misinformed and anxious. Below, I have listed some difficult issues to reflect on when talking to children about crisis situations; I have COVID-19 in mind, but this can equally be applied to many other scenarios.

Issue 1

The difficulty of helping children to be open and see the good in neighbours and strangers combined with the necessity of keeping physical distance.

I think that this is an extremely difficult balance to maintain as we need children to be wary of strangers and neighbours (and friends and family!), including other children and animals, in terms of maintaining distance, but we also want them to keep an open mind and not be overwhelmed by 'stranger danger'. I would suggest making a visual representation of the distance that needs to be kept from others with masking tape on the floor and reminding children why this needs to happen. We need to model this for children when out and make it easier for them by keeping them with us so that they aren't so exposed to seeing adults swerving away from them.

We can also make sure that they see us wave and smile at people so that they understand that the distance is not because of anything to do with that person; it is solely because of the virus, and the person is still friendly. An interesting and helpful idea is to think of 'physical' distancing rather than 'social' distancing, and to use this term with children. If they hear the adult say 'I'm physically distancing from you, not social distancing because I want to say "Hello", but from a safe distance' then the idea that we remain friends and neighbours whilst staying away from each other temporarily for all of our safety can be reinforced in a positive way.

We should also make clear to children that we are keeping our distance because of our danger to others as well as their danger to us. I think that this two-way emphasis really helps children to see that the outside world is not a unilateral threat, and that we all have to work hard to protect each other. Some family members and friends, in particular grandparents, older relatives or those with underlying health issues, may be particularly vulnerable and it is important that children understand this.

Issue 2

The difficulty of making sure that children understand the severity of the situation while still reassuring them that they are safe and the adults around them are working hard to keep them safe.

This can apply to any crisis situation. Children will know that this period of time isn't life as they have known it and they will want explanations as to why this is. Again, parents, carers and practitioners will know their own children and will understand what individually and age-appropriate terms to use and the details of what conversations to have. We would stress that parents need to put their own anxieties aside in order to reassure children when talking to them. Goldman (2001) uses some good phrases, and a starting point can be to reassure children by talking about the brave people who are working hard to keep us safe.

Parents can also emphasise that everyone is trying to stay safe and talk about hand washing and physical distancing as examples of good practice. This empowers children and reminds them that they can be active and play a part in keeping themselves safe. Taking cues from a child when discussing a crisis situation is important. Asking them what they know and whether there's anything they're worried about is a good starting point. Take your lead from them.

In any situation it's important for parents to have a conversation, if at all possible, away from their own anxieties and in a calm manner. Some of the most revealing conversations with children happen when doing an activity with them rather than 'having a talk'. When hands are busy with play dough, junk modelling or sticking it takes the stress out of a situation and children feel more able to talk about any fears and worries they might have, rather than being sat down and asked directly – that can seem very worrying to a young child.

The good stuff

I think that there is good stuff to be found in the present situation. I'm in touch with a former student who is on complete lockdown in Italy at this moment; she says that she gets excited taking the out rubbish and recycling, whereas previously it was a chore! I am sure that we've all found interest in small things as the pace of our life has slowed down. I look forward to my one walk each day, and notice much more in my patio as I spend more time outside and look more closely.

I have focused on the negative aspects of a family being forced to spend more time together, but there are positives too. Parents have told me how much they appreciate not having to rush for the school run, being more involved in their children's learning, having time to spend on ongoing art projects and tapping into their own creativity in order to support their children.

The result of this might be a new hobby for the family or new rituals and routines that can be sustained after the crisis has passed. It might be that the adults and children are making time to talk more openly about their feelings and what is difficult for them. Families might exercise together more whereas previously they did this separately. They might watch an exercise video together or go for a bike ride. Prior to lockdown, parents would have left much of this activity up to the school or nursery to arrange. Now it is something that they have to do together.

Parents who usually work long hours away from the home are working at home and so have their usual commuting time to spend with their children. Life isn't so rushed for some people. Of course, I can't let this comment go by without reflecting that for many of the people working in front-line services life is busier than ever. This includes those who have volunteered or returned to caring work.

There are also a huge amount of local caring groups and forums that have been set up. Today alone, there have been many messages and offers of help in my area: a local firm making natural body products wanted to donate some to health workers who are continually washing their hands, while someone else has cooked too much vegan and vegetarian food and wants to know if anyone wants any. Crisis situations can bring out the best in people, and the bulk of the population are responding in a generally responsible and proactive way.

We hope that these connections last after the crisis has passed. Many online groups are talking about street parties when possible. Having close local relationships can only be beneficial for children in the long term. It might be that, pre-crisis, their parent(s) had no local support and now they have found some. They might meet other children in the area, even at a distance. Certainly through the groups that are springing up in this situation children are receiving the message that adults can be kind and helpful and reach out to strangers for no reward other than to help and to feel useful.

There are very few people for whom life is easy at the moment, and that includes those without children. A friend remarked to me that this was a great leveller and that she did feel a sense of 'we're all in this together'. Of course, I would be naïve if I didn't acknowledge that privilege, money and status go some way towards easing the difficulties that we are all facing. A large house with a big garden will make childcare and education easier than a small flat with no outside space. Money will also allow access to online resources that will help. Good Wi-Fi, sophisticated computers and access to Netflix, etc., will help entertain and instruct children.

Those parents able to share not only the childcare, education and household jobs but also the worry and organisation with each other will also gain. It might be that this crisis has forced parents to look at their high-paced lifestyle and reconsider how they live their lives – this will ultimately have a positive effect on family life.

Being in lockdown might bring families closer as they participate in joint activities. In childcare and education we generally see children divided by age, and the current situation can mean that siblings have to spend more time together. This may cause conflict, but it can also bring nearness as older and younger children play games together and interact – even if it's just watching a TV programme together. It might be that parents are generally not able to spend much time with their children due to the demands of work, perhaps a caring role for a grandparent, and social and household tasks.

This time throws families together: parent(s) with each other, parent(s) with children and children with each other. This can cause conflict, but also closeness and special family time. Some families have reported that children are generally less stressed and more relaxed away from the pressures of formal school time.

Contact with extended family and friends during a lockdown period will mostly be online, but this can mean that there is more interaction than usual even if it is virtual contact. People might be making a greater effort to stay in touch and provide support to their circle of family and friends.

Case study 7.1

Lola (age six) is in lockdown with her older brother, mother and father. Her school is closed and this is day two of homeschooling. Just as she is about to go to bed she realises that she can't find her reading diary and becomes distressed and upset. Her mother tries to reassure her that as she isn't at school at the moment she doesn't need it but Lola is inconsolable. Lola's older brother, Ben, makes fun of Lola's distress; she becomes very aggressive with him and blames him for the loss of the book. She also shouts at her mother and blames her for the whole lockdown situation.

Reflections

Lola's mother had to deal with this situation at the end of the day, a time when there are often flashpoints as everyone is tired and sensitive. Because of this fairly new situation there was even more tension in the air and Lola's mother could see that the situation was about to escalate into full-scale conflict. She was struggling with her own tiredness and anxiety and was very upset that Lola had blamed her for a situation that was beyond her control. She asked Ben to leave his sister alone and go to his room, and suggested that he played with a toy he especially liked. She sat with Lola, waited until she had calmed down and explained to her that she would look for the book first thing the next day but that now it was time to go to sleep.

Lola seemed to be upset over a trivial matter. In fact, this was just a token, a symbol of a deeper upset. Her whole routine had been upset as she wasn't able to go to school and it was significant that losing something that was so integral to her school day had been the catalyst for her upset. It was also noteworthy that this happened at the end of the day. Lola had managed to keep her emotions in check throughout the day, but at the end of it, when she was tired and her defences were down, she was triggered by this sense of loss and felt overwhelming upset.

Earlier in the day, when asked by her parents how she felt, Lola had seemed bright and happy and said that she loved being away from school and didn't find the lockdown at all worrying.

This shows us that a sense of loss can attach itself to a minor detail but actually may be about something much deeper.

Case study 7.2

Barnaby is six and his brother, Jacob, is five. They were asked what they found difficult about the lockdown. They said that they were worried about their aunty being on her own as they used to see her once a week. They speak to her on Facetime but miss her a lot. They also miss their teachers and friends and especially miss playing in the playground.

Their mother and father are worried about finances as they're both self-employed and also have concerns for their parents' and relatives' safety. They are finding homeschooling difficult but are enjoying the involvement in their children's learning and appreciating having more time for projects without the continual rush to get to school and other clubs and events. Having more time means they can take longer making and creating things, and they feel that they are listening, engaging and having fun together.

Reflections on homeschooling during a crisis

I saw an online post that said 'You are not working from home; you are at your home during a crisis trying to work'. I think that this could be applied to homeschooling children and dealing with this unprecedented situation. Basically, we're all doing the best that we can and we can't recreate 'normal' life for children, whatever that may be. We note that many children are homeschooled in a non-crisis situation and that this is done very successfully. We are not trying to say that homeschooling is a 'lesser' system than school. What we are saying is that during standard homeschooling children can go out and visit museums and other places of interest, and they can meet other children and join in group activities with other homeschooled children. It is true that in this scenario those who homeschool are probably better equipped to deal with this system than others, but even for them homeschooling will look different.

All we can do is set up our own routines and help children feel secure and loved. By lessening the pressure to make every minute a formal school day we can notice the benefits of a lockdown situation and also create a sustainable nurturing and relaxed atmosphere at home.

Case study 7.3

Emma is the parent of Lucy, aged four. They have a very close relationship with Emma's mother, Jacky, who lives in the same street as them and usually provides a lot of childcare support. Jacky is having to shield and stay in her home as she is very vulnerable due to health issues. Emma and Lucy wave at Jacky through the window but afterwards Emma is always very upset that she cannot go into her grandmother's house and hug her. Emma decides that perhaps it's better not to see Jacky in order to avoid these tears.

Reflections

While everyone has to make up their own mind about what they can cope with, here it is Emma's upset at Lucy's tears that is the greatest obstacle. It is reasonable for Lucy to be upset and she needs support with that. She also needs continuity, and seeing her grandmother, even in a limited way, will help to provide that. Emma could facilitate this further, perhaps with Zoom bedtime stories and holding up signs and pictures for Jacky to read and she do the same. Emma is also upset by her own lack of physical contact with Jacky, though she is denying this because she is focusing on Lucy's feelings. In this situation it would be good to admit that they are both sad and missing Jacky.

The future

Because a crisis situation is so awful and stressful, after it has passed there can be a tendency to try to go back to 'normal' life as quickly as possible and, in doing so, 'pretend' that the situation didn't happen in an attempt to negate its effects. We understand and sympathise with this reasoning. In fact, in the same way as after bereavement, life after a crisis situation will never be the same. One obvious and sad reason is that there may have been an associated bereavement or extended period of sickness of the child or people around them.

But even without the crisis dramatically affecting a child in this way, there will always be the memory of the difficult time, and this needs to be spoken about and talked through in order to prevent future problems. The child needs to be given age-appropriate information before, during and after the crisis, and it is important for the adults around them to communicate honestly in order for the child to adapt to and cope with change. This applies to changes both during the crisis and afterwards.

The effects of the crisis could be extended in terms of economics. The parents might have lost their jobs, or they might both need to work rather than just one of them. They might not be able to afford daycare outside the home, out-of-school clubs or private school any longer. All of this will affect a child's life after the crisis. Goods and services might be limited for a while after the crisis. There might still be some form of restrictions in place. A child needs to be involved in conversations about this and about how the future will look. Of course, these conversations need to be in line with their age and level of understanding.

There might also be good things after a crisis. A family might feel closer and have stronger links with family, friends and neighbours. They might feel more connected to their local community because of the help they were offered or offered to others. These are positive effects from a crisis that it is good to note with the child. In that way they learn to understand that life and the people around them are multi-faceted and that there are shades of grey between 'good' and 'bad'.

Key ideas from this chapter

- Feelings of loss can be masked by a smaller grief.
- Every parent and child is doing the best that they can under difficult situations.
- Aspects of crisis situations can be universal.
- Each family finds its own solutions to the difficulties, and these will vary.
- Keeping to routines (albeit new routines) will reassure and empower children.

Reference

Goldman, L. (2001) *Breaking the Silence*. London: Routledge.

8 | Ways forward and conclusion

For the final part of this book we want to draw together the main points, and also have a look at some specific and more focused areas of supporting children with feelings of grief and loss, including using resources such as books and films and working with children with special needs.

We opened by saying that one of our aims in writing this book was to produce a resource so that early years practitioners and parents/carers are prepared in advance for children with strong feelings of loss or grief. Of course, it might be that the reader is turning to this book because of a crisis situation, and in this case we are pleased that the information herein may be helpful and supportive. Ideally, though, this book should be a useful resource for practitioners and others to use in a more general way. We found that many of the participants of our one-day grief and loss training attended because of an immediate crisis or difficulties in their setting. Because of this they had to 'hit the ground running' in terms of trying to make sense of the training in relation to the problem that they needed to address. They then returned to the setting to put some of the training into immediate practice. We were concerned that, because of the difficulties in the setting, the rest of the staff team who had not attended the training might not fully understand the reasoning behind some of the initiatives and practices and that the messages from the training could be diluted or misinterpreted by hasty implementation. There would be little time for the staff team to reflect on and discuss the information from the training. In order to support staff teams, in Appendix C we have provided some ideas for how to structure staff training sessions on working with children with feelings of loss and grief; these ideas can be delivered in different sequences and in a range of time slots in order to accommodate a range of training situations. We realise that having a whole day for training is an infeasible luxury for many settings and sometimes there may just be a two-hour slot after the setting has closed for the day, or perhaps a morning or afternoon.

Having an idea of how to support children with feelings of grief and loss and making this work as a cornerstone of daily practice will not only ensure a healthier and more nurturing environment for the children in the setting, but will also be empowering for the adults around them, including parents and carers. In order to enable the children to feel secure and to be able to express their feelings more fully, the adults in the setting need to model this so as to set a good example. If children are able to express their feelings and have them witnessed and listened to, then this practice will also extend to the adults in the setting. This will foster a better working environment for the staff team and also, by extension, for the parents and carers who use the facility. This respectful engagement with and nurturing of feelings within staff teams and between staff and children should benefit the whole setting and the families who are connected with it.

Children with special needs

We are not suggesting that there should be any additional or different support for children with special needs than would be provided for any other child. In fact, a programme of support for a child with special needs is exactly the same as for any child in that it needs to be individualised to that particular child's needs, taking account of their age, stage of development and understanding, and their interests. Hence, it might be the case that a child with special needs would need that same support and help broken down more by an adult in order for it to be more accessible to them.

We would also ask you to think about the vast array of different needs in terms of emotional literacy that children have. Assuming that because a child has special needs they would need extra help accessing this emotional work is not always accurate. In the same way, a child who is developmentally within or above what is expected for their age might not have the emotional insight to understand the ideas about feelings and emotions that we discuss here. Ultimately, what we are saying is that each child is an individual, and their particular needs and interests need to be assessed in order to make the emotional support that you offer them meaningful and targeted.

A setting that is able to provide appropriate support for both the youngest and the oldest of the children that it cares for will have a wide range of suitable strategies and ways of helping children that can be adapted to meet the needs of all of the children who use that setting.

It may be that a child is not able to verbalise fully, perhaps because of their age or due to their stage of development. In this case, the practitioner needs to observe the child using all of the workers' senses and skills, and then direct their support accordingly. They might use fewer or simpler words, and/or signs and touch to provide emotional support. The younger a child is the more they will explore the world in a sensory way and also use sensory experiences to comfort themselves, such as rubbing silky labels or touching particular materials – for example, a blanket or special toy. They might also suck their thumb or fingers or perform other repetitive behaviours. This may also be true for a child with special needs, but it would really depend on the child's individual behaviours and we would hope that the key worker of the child would know them well enough not to assume that they might not have feelings of grief and loss because of their special needs.

Thinking about fantasy

Young children may be less able to distinguish between fantasy and the real world. As adults we have clear ideas about what is 'real' and what isn't. The idea of death and loss can seem like another fantasy story to small children. We have to remember that we continually tell young children stories that contain fantasy elements; this might include well-loved figures such as the tooth fairy, Father Christmas, the Easter Bunny and other culturally linked fantasy figures. Why, then, should a child not think that someone dying is yet another such story? They may not have clear ideas regarding the scope and details of what an adult may or may not be able to do. They might also find it hard to understand our limitations – i.e. what it is and is not possible for humans to do. In a child's eyes, it may be that adults are capable of anything, including the impossible. A colleague of mine has a son who has special needs and when his father died he couldn't understand why they couldn't just go to visit him. His mother had told him that his father had gone to heaven. In the son's mind, this was just another place that they could go to, and his mother would be capable of taking him if she chose to. In order to fully support a young child we need to try and see the world through their eyes, and this is especially true when working with children with special needs.

> In responding to needs of the young child, the caregiver must provide an emotional sense of comfort, love, warmth, attention and acceptance. In other words, the process of helping the child cope with the loss demands a 'helping-healing-adult' who can provide the emotional support and care necessary
>
> (Wolfelt, 1983, p. 30)

Stars in the sky

Something that we have increasingly seen being used is the concept that a loved family member, friend or pet has gone to the sky and is now a star in the sky. This can bring great comfort to families, and as it is not linked to any religious ideology it is often used as a secular way of thinking that the dead are still present and looking over us.

We have no objection to this as long as it is handled sensitively and is perhaps something the child and parent talk about together and mark with an activity. For example: they might go outside, look up at the night sky and use it as a time to remember someone or something that has gone. They might draw pictures of the sky and the star in it.

We would say that this has to be explained fully as misunderstandings can easily occur. A child needs to understand that we can't go up into the sky and visit the dead person (not even in an airplane), but that they are there and still care for us, and we still think of them. A friend who has a son with special needs in his early twenties used this successfully when the young man was deeply affected by the death of his grandfather, with whom he had a very special relationship. Once he understood that he couldn't go and visit his grandfather in the star he took great comfort from the idea of his grandfather as a star in the sky and referred to it often. Special care might be needed for the part of the idea that refers to the departed person looking down on the child. They might find that ominous and be troubled by it: 'They look down on me all the time? They see everything I do?' The adult would have to be very sensitive and carefully convey the feeling that this is a general idea of being aware of the child but not overlooking their day-to-day life.

We have also heard of the idea of finding a feather, sometimes a white one, from a loved one who has died. When children find feathers, the parent tells them that it's a message from the missed person. Again, this needs to be handled sensitively, but it can be a lovely thought. And it's amazing how many feathers do come into our lives!

Reading books with children

At the end of the book we have included appendices with ideas for accompanying resources and activities that you can use alongside this book and in your work with children. The following section looks more closely at some of the books that you could use. Before we detail this, we wanted to examine some of the ideas you might consider when reading with children generally in order to fully support any discussions you might have.

Educate or entertain?

It's adults who mainly write, produce, sell and choose books for children. This isn't the place to look at this process in detail, or at the history of why and what we have produced for children to read. We have included a useful book about children's literature in the references at the end of this chapter if you are interested in examining this in more detail. However, here it is worth outlining some of the main ideas in order to understand the purpose of the books that we choose. The tension in books for children has always been between using books as a tool for education or simply to entertain and interest children. The earliest books for children were generally there to teach them the alphabet or religious content. There was then a move towards books that had a strong moral code or message, which includes fairy tales. Think about 'Little Red Riding Hood': that story has changed a lot since its inception, but the basic message is the same – always a version of 'Don't stray off the path and be careful because the world is full of danger'. Examining text and pictures for the message that the book contains is even more relevant when thinking about books that include themes of grief and loss. Within the story there will be something that is underpinning it. It is so important that we read the books first and fully understand the message that they are giving to children. As adults, we have to understand and be able to discuss what the book is saying to the child; this discussion could be the cornerstone of further interesting conversations with the child about their understanding of any message.

I would also note that even when we are looking at books that purport only to entertain, there might be a message in the book that comes from the author's own moral code and that of the society around them at the time of writing. It is very hard to separate the writing from the author's point of view and their background, as this will be what frames their writing.

Think about how differently childhood is portrayed in books through the ages and where that detail comes from. The case of what children in the book are allowed to do by adults is a good starting point. As an illustration, the children in E. Nesbit's books are able to travel and roam freely around London in a way that would not be considered acceptable today. All of this detail comes from the author's own experiences and what was considered common practice at the time, and this is included in the books.

So, it is our responsibility to carefully examine the books that we read with young children and to understand the obvious messages in the book, as well as those that might be more deeply buried but are still there.

Moving onto those books that entertain, just for interest the first published book for children that is recognised as aiming to entertain without an overt and direct moral message is *Alice's Adventures in Wonderland* by Lewis Carroll (1865). It is crucial when we are looking for books to read to children that contain elements of grief and loss that they also have an interesting and lively storyline so that children are involved in them. Books that are 'all message' can be dull, and because of that they are ineffectual. We would recommend Letterbox Library (www.Letterboxlibrary.com) as a source for books that have been carefully vetted to ensure that they educate and entertain as well as being diverse and inclusive. Below we look at a variety of classic and more current children's books that one might not immediately think of as containing elements of grief and loss.

Death, accidents and sickness in children's fiction

The main source for this section is Lois Keith's excellent book, *Take up thy Bed and Walk* (2001). Children's books written in the past (we're thinking mainly of Victorian and Edwardian fiction) often featured an orphan as the main child protagonist. This could be because of the higher rate of postnatal death at the time or because, without overseeing parents, the adventures that the child entered into were more accessible. In addition, when we think of children's adventures most of them happen in the school holidays, when children would have more freedom and less structure to their day. A notable exception of course is the boarding school genre, such as the *Harry Potter* series, where the adventures mostly happen at school. Examples of classic fiction where children are orphaned or apart from their parents are: *The Secret Garden, A Little Princess, Heidi, What Katy Did* (her father is alive), *Pollyanna, Ballet Shoes, Anne of Green Gables, The BFG, Storm Breaker, Charmed Life, The Jungle Book* and *Jane Eyre*. In the *Narnia* books the children are away from their parents for their adventures in Narnia; at the very end of the series (spoiler) the children 'die' in a train accident but are then transported to Narnia. I must also mention here *Tom's Midnight Garden*, as in this book Tom has to go and stay with his aunt and uncle because of measles in his home. This would be a good book to read with children during the current pandemic, as there are many comparisons to be drawn. Tom also has very strong feelings about his situation, and discussion of his thoughts would be a good way of getting an insight into a child's feelings about the crisis.

Of course, some classic children's books featured scenarios where the children had parents and lived with them, but despite this they were mainly cared for by nannies and other staff. Examples of this would be *Peter Pan* (the nanny is a dog), *Swallows and Amazons*, and *Five Children and It*, amongst many others.

In addition to the loss of parents, books may feature the loss of a sibling; the most well-known example of this is the death of Beth in *Little Women*. Or they could feature a near-death accident: again *Heidi*, with her friend Clara; *Little Women*, with Amy nearly drowning when skating; and Katy in *What Katy Did* and the rest of the series. In these books there is sometimes the possibility of a 'miracle cure', which reinforces our point about children getting confused about what is and is not possible and what is really within an adult's power.

These books have been more widely read by older generations than by present-day children, and a thought to consider is that reading these books could have shaped the way a generation thinks about death, and that this has been carried over to future generations. The messages that these books contained can still be seen in some contemporary children's fiction: for example, the 'near death' experience. To illustrate this, Harry Potter briefly visits death near the end of the series, but then comes back from the dead and returns to Hogwarts for the finale. There are also many TV series where characters miraculously return from the dead, and hence the distinction between reality and fantasy can get blurred in a child's mind, especially when such events happen in real-life settings rather than fantastical ones.

All of this blurs the distinction between what is real, what is possible and what is not, and as adults we have to be prepared for children to not understand the finality of some losses. Again, we would question whether even as 'grown ups' we can truly understand that when a loved one dies they are physically gone forever and that we will never see them again. One of our primary views in this book is that, as adults, we hope to be able to answer all of our children's questions and to allay their fears with our superior knowledge. But death is a great mystery. We might have a faith or other way of making sense of what happens when we die. Ultimately, though, we cannot fully answer children's questions or reassure them completely. In a child's mind, death can be as great a fantasy as *Harry Potter* or *Peter Pan*. As Peter Pan himself famously says, 'Death is an awfully big adventure.' For your interest, this line was taken out when Peter Pan was performed as a pantomime during wartime. It is also one to watch out for if reading to a child or watching the film, especially if the child has experienced a bereavement.

Reading books to children

Case study 8.1

This is a true story. In a day nursery, a group of children (aged 3) have a few minutes before getting coats on and being picked up by their parents and carers. The key worker gathers them together in a room. They sit on the floor in a circle, and she starts to read a book that she has picked at random from a pile. The book contains a story about a child who has a pet hamster that has died. One child in the group puts up their hand and asks 'What does 'die' mean?' The practitioner is slightly flustered by this question and, after hesitating, replies 'That's a very interesting question and I don't think I've got time to answer it today. Maybe we can think about it tomorrow.' She then continues with the story. The book carries on to explain that the boy with the hamster is very sad because his pet has died and isn't with him anymore. A different child asks 'Why is the boy sad? Where has his hamster gone?' The children ask more questions and there is a feeling of heightened anxiety in the room.

What would you do in this situation? What words would you use to the child?

When this incident took place I was carrying out a local authority inspection of this setting, and the practitioner was so upset and nervous that I went into another room while she dealt with the situation so that she so she didn't feel she was 'on the spot', so I didn't actually hear how it was resolved. Afterwards, I gently suggested to her that she might want to read a book herself before she reading it to the children; she agreed.

As you can see from this example, books always need to be read by adults before they are read to children so that this sort of situation can be anticipated. This also underpins our point that these books shouldn't be used in response to a crisis situation, but to prepare in advance for the questions that children will have. In this way the children will be used to the books and relaxed about seeing them around, rather than disturbed or frightened by them. The adults will know that this book might raise such questions and will be better prepared to answer them. Of course, because of difficult questions practitioners might make a conscious decision not to have this type of book out in the general resource area and decide to save it for a particular situation. This might be because they feel unprepared to answer questions. We would argue that it is important for the book to be out so that grief and loss are seen as natural and a part of everyday life – not something new and possibly scary.

When we were delivering equalities training we would suggest that the books that were chosen in a setting should reflect the diversity of the world around the children. Practitioners would sometimes say 'Oh, but we haven't got any children who are culturally diverse attending the session'. We would point out that the children in the nursery will grow up and venture into a much wider world, and it is healthy for them to see that world represented positively in their early years.

In the same way, there might be a time when practitioners are not aware of any child who is experiencing feelings of grief and loss (although we are not always aware of this). However, we don't know when such a situation might arise, so if children are already familiar with these concepts through books it paves the way for more specific discussions as and when a child has their own experience of loss and grief that they want to discuss. Using a book as an entry point can be very useful. For example, a widely used book such as *Badgers Parting Gifts* can be referred to by the practitioner 'Remember when we read…' 'Be prepared' is our guideline here.

As well as reading books in advance, there are also some films that should be watched by adults before children see them. If this isn't possible, adults at least need to read the reviews and ask other people for their opinion on the film's content. Too often when something is classified as suitable for children (we're not just talking censor ratings here), the finer points of plot are overlooked. It might also be that a child is sensitised to certain subjects because of recent events in their lives, and so films that would be enjoyable for one child would be traumatic for another. Of course, watching a film purposefully because it contains sensitive material would require time afterwards to discuss this and deal with any questions raised by the child. Classic films that we know to contain such material are:

Watership Down
The *Harry Potter* series (the later ones especially)
Bambi (original Disney)
Dumbo (original Disney)

The Secret Garden (Mary is an orphan)
A Little Princess (the book is different, as in the film the father has just lost his memory and not died)
Peter Pan

See Appendix A for more helpful materials. We have also included some additional suggestions for books and films to use with children or to be aware of.

Conclusion

We hope that by reading this book and reflecting on the case studies that we have included you have gained a fuller understanding of how best to support children with feelings of grief after bereavement, as well as with more general feelings of loss. We also hope that you have gained a personal awareness of loss in all its many forms, how these might feel for a child and how this might differ for an adult. You should also have some ideas about how to understand and support children when they have these feelings, and the many different ways that they might express them.

In conclusion, there are two main points that we would like to make: first, we cannot minimise how children feel. To put it bluntly – and also to reiterate, as we have made this important point throughout the book – just because children are physically little, it does not mean that they have little feelings. We need to have an eye to the future and to the children's journey into adulthood. We need to understand that if very young children are not supported well with these feelings by the adults around them, the feelings do not go away; they can be carried throughout life and affect children as they move through the difficult time of puberty and beyond. Even with support, we cannot guarantee that these strong feelings will not return in different ways.

These feelings of loss and grief can also be revisited at different times in someone's life. It is also true that an incident or loss that may seem minor can then trigger bigger feelings of grief and loss that we have experienced in the past. For example, I find that if I am at a funeral, even if I was not especially close to that person, my grief can be very intense as it reminds me of other funerals and people close to me that have left my life. These feelings are circular and can be revisited again and again. As we note throughout this book, they become part of the fabric of our life rather than something we 'get over', discard and forget.

As an example of this, I was teaching a class of mature students; we were discussing the language we use with children and how we ensure that we speak to them respect-fully. One student, a woman in her 60s, she recounted how a teacher had told her that she was 'stupid' when she was at infant school. As she told the story we could all clearly see and feel the pain and bitterness in her voice and face. She was at a workshop for people who had not proceeded to higher education in their teenage years and wanted to return to study and gain a degree while working in early years education. I sensed that the teacher's comment had really affected this student's perception of herself and her intelligence, and that she had carried this with her for a long time. It was possible that it had held her back from exploring the opportunities that were available to her because she had internalised those thoughtless and cruel words and felt that she was 'stupid' and not able to study and learn.

I also believe that, while it's important to be aware of the significance of our words and actions with children, as parents and carers we do the best that we can in any situation and shouldn't load ourselves with guilt. We do have to see that a child's expression of pain at any loss is their experience and is valid. As adults we find it hard to witness children's feelings of upset and we do everything that we can to stop them feeling sad. We give them distractions – sweets, toys – and sometimes, because of our own stress and upset, we say harsh words to children in order to achieve that aim. I remember as a child being told that if I wouldn't be quiet, I'd be given something to cry about. Ultimately, sometimes we just have to be with children, listen to their pain and give them love and support that way. This is easy to say but hard to do consistently, especially when we, the adult in the situation, feel upset and like a child ourselves. We think that parents, carers and practitioners do a wonderful job with children and ultimately want what's best for them. We cannot always act in the way that we know is best practice, but we do the best we can.

The second and final point we want to make is to reiterate that, as adults, we are the ones in charge, the people who are in control. To children, we appear to have all of the power and all of the answers. In terms of grief and loss, we don't always have control or know the answers. We cannot make things better all of the time or give full reassurance. The only reassurance we can give is that we love the child and that we are there for them. That is our main – and our most important – job.

References

Alcott, L. M. (1873) *Little Women; or, Meg, Jo, Beth, and Amy*. London: George Routledge.

Barrie, J. M. (1900) *Peter Pan*. Oxford: Oxford University Press.

Bronte, C. (1847) *Jane Eyre*. New York: John W. Lovell Co.

Burnett, F. H. (1900) *The Secret Garden*. London: Walker Books.

Burnett, F. H., & Piffard, H. (1900) *A Little Princess: Being the Whole Story of Sara Crewe, Now Told for the First Time*. London: F. Warne.

Coolidge, S. (1800) *What Katy Did: A Story,* London: Ward, Lock, and Co., Warwick House.

Horowitz, A. (2000) *Alex Rider*. New York: Philomel Books.

Jones, D. W., & Stevens, T. (2000) *Charmed Life*. London: Collins.

Keith, L. (2001) *Take up Thy Bed and Walk*. London: The Women's Press.

Montgomery, L. M. (1900) *Anne of Green Gables*. Garden City, NY: International Collectors Library.

Nesbit, E. (1900) *Five Children and It*. New York: Coward.

Pearce, P. (1959) *Tom's Midnight Garden*. Oxford: Oxford University Press.

Ransome, A. (1930) *Swallows and Amazons*. London: J. Cape.

Rowling, J. K. (1997) *Harry Potter and the Philosopher's Stone*. London: Bloomsbury.

Spyri, J. (1956) *Heidi*. Harmondsworth: Penguin.

Streatfield, N. (1900) *Ballet Shoes: A Story of Three Children on the Stage*. Harmondsworth: Penguin.

Varley, S. (1992) *Badger's Parting Gifts*. London: HarperCollins.

Wolfelt, A. (1983) *Helping Children Cope with Grief*. Abingdon: Routledge.

Appendix A
Book list

In early years settings we use books as a tool to begin conversations. We find that it is easier, more natural and less intimidating than sitting a child down and 'having a chat'. This is especially relevant when wanting to talk about feelings of grief and loss.

Reading these books together just once may be all that is needed. Or it may be that it could take many attempts over many days to help children to understand what has happened, be it a death, moving house, missing friends – any type of change in circumstances or coping with 'big feelings' they may not yet understand or have the words for.

It is good practice to read these books to yourself initially and consider the possible questions or emotions they will stir up. This way you will be better prepared to work through both the story and any associated issues with the children in your care. This gives you the opportunity to question how you feel and to examine how the story affects you. To this day, I am unable to read aloud one of the books on this list because it renders me speechless with well-hidden grief, sadness and upset. If you too are faced with strong, personal, even historic feelings, then acknowledge those feelings, seek help if needed and move on to a different book which will be less pertinent to you.

We suggest leaving the books in the staff room for casual browsing. This can then be a 'door opener' for the adults, and an acknowledgement that in order to support children through their strong feelings, the adults have to think about their emotions too. This also enables the team to read them through without the immediate pressure of having to read with the children. In reading them, individuals can informally ask a colleague what they thought about details of a book and this helps practitioners gain confidence.

If anyone in the team has strong opinions about any of the books, it is best to find out before they are used with the children. I have had some of these books thrown at me as being 'inappropriate' for use with young children. On unpicking that particularly fraught interaction, the workers felt that children should be protected from death at all costs – something that, in our opinion, is unwise and unhelpful, as discussed at length throughout this book.

Books for young children about bereavement

Always and Forever, *Gliori, D., and Durant, A. (2013) London: Picture Corgi*

Otter, Mole, Fox and Hare live together as a family, but Fox dies: '…a wintry sadness settled on the house in the woods.' Time passes, and over dinner one day they start to talk about all the things they miss about Fox. 'And in their hearts and their memories and their laughter, Fox was still there…always and forever.' This is not a book to use in the first few weeks of grief but a helpful story to read one-to-one or in a small group. A great 'door opener' even if no one in the nursery is currently coping with a bereavement. We would say that this is one for the regular bookshelf.

Badger's Parting Gifts, *Varley, S. (2019) London: Anderson Press*

This is an old favourite and one of the only books we have found that has been translated into some community languages. Badger is old and does his best to prepare his friends for his death. 'Fox broke the sad news that Badger was dead': This is a book for young children that actually uses the word 'dead'. Each of the animals had a special memory of Badger, of something he taught them that they could now do extremely well: 'He had given them each a parting gift to treasure always.' We would suggest that this is another regular 'bookshelf book', useful to open up a conversation about death at circle time.

The Invisible String, *Karst, P. (2019) New York: Little Brown and Company*

'And the twins are told to go back to bed even though they are scared.' This is a useful book that covers separation anxiety, loss and grief. We are still connected to the people we love even when we are apart, because love connects us like an invisible string. Heaven is mentioned, but this line could be omitted when reading the story if preferred. Read it through first and omit those parts that you do not deem helpful, or keep them in as preferred. The same author has produced an *Invisible String* workbook and two other books: *The Invisible Leash*, which is about a pet dying; and *The Invisible Web*, which is about love and universal connection.

I Miss You, *Thomas, P. and Harker, L. (2017) London: Wayland*

This has simple text and illustrations, and takes an honest look at feelings, being sensibly and kindly written by Pat Thomas, a psychotherapist and counsellor. This is one of the few books that mentions funerals, especially within the context of different beliefs. There is a helpful section on how to use the book at home or in pre-school/school. It is our most popular book in the toy library on this topic, and the go-to book for families as soon as they feel able to read it at home. If nursery funds are tight, buy two copies of this: one for the children and one to lend the family. It helpfully covers all aspects of death that we have been asked about by early years settings. Thomas has also written a book called *I Miss My Pet*, which addresses the death of a family pet.

Granpa, *Burningham, J. (2003) London: Jonathan Cope*

This is a beautifully illustrated and gentle book about Granpa and his granddaughter, who have a lovely, fun and playful relationship. After scenes of them playing together and going to the beach, it then shows that Granpa is too poorly to play; the final picture is his empty chair. It's hard for anyone reading this who has had a similar experience not to get upset, but crying is healthy and can comfort some children with the realisation that they are not alone, and you feel the same as they do.

Liplap's Wish, *London, J. and Long, S. (1994) New York: Scholastic*

This is a beautifully illustrated book. Liplap the rabbit makes his first snow bunny and realises that his Grandma is no longer there to see it. His mother gently tells him the rabbit legend: 'when the first rabbits died they became stars in the sky…and to this day they come out at night to watch over us. And they remind us that our loved ones shine forever in our hearts. That's why we wish upon a star.' We've found this to be a very popular book for adults to read to children, mainly because it perpetuates the comforting idea that our dear departed still shine down on us as stars, and thus can still be part of our lives. This story leaves us with an affirmation, as opposed to the bleakness left behind with some others.

When Dinosaurs Die, *Krasny Brown, L. and Brown, M. (2009) New York: Little, Brown and Company*

This is a book that evokes strong feelings. Some practitioners like it because it covers both feelings and the logistics of death; others dislike it because it is too 'wordy' and covers too much. It is helpful that it features the dinosaur family because they are one step removed from a human family and so can be especially useful when your setting encompasses many cultures. You can leave out irrelevant sections (e.g. those about suicide and cremation). We would not say that this is a bedtime book, but a useful catch-all for the bookshelf. It is especially helpful for ages eight and upwards, in our opinion, because all the facts are there and it has enough detail for a confident reader. If you are using it in a nursery, it is especially important to read it first and adapt it to suit your group's needs. Dinosaurs are often very popular with children because they are fascinated by them, and so they will usually sit for long enough to do this book justice and ask endless questions about the dinosaur family, which at the same time enables the practitioner to also talk about the topic.

Water Bugs and Dragonflies, *Stickney, D. (1982) Cleveland, OH: Pilgrim Press*

This is a simple tale of the circle of life and has been in use since the 1970s. It explains to children how water bugs become dragonflies and then die, and why you cannot see your deceased loved ones again. We feel it contains helpful advice for adults on how to use the book. The underpinning messages have a Christian slant, so this is something to be aware of when using it.

Lifetimes, *Mellonie, B. (1983) New York: Bantam*

'There are lots of living things in our world. Each one has its own special lifetime.' This wonderfully illustrated book tells children of all ages (and adults, too) about beginnings, endings and everything in between. It contains plants, animals and people, and provides gentle but factual explanations of different lifespans. Since the book was first written in 1983, the human life span has increased by nearly 20 years, and this is something to consider if grandparents are reading this to their families. It is non-religious, and we think it is one for the nursery bookshelf. We would especially recommend looking at Chapter 5 in terms of using this book when there are dead flowers or dead flies on the nursery window ledge.

Muddles, Puddles and Sunshine: Your Activity Book to Help When Someone Has Died, *Sheppard, K. and Crossley, D. (2000) Winston's Wish, Stroud, Hawthorn Press*

This book suggests helpful activities and exercises as an outlet for the difficult feelings following the death of someone special. We feel that it is best suited to ages five and over. We would suggest that you read it at nursery in order to get some ideas of activities to do with a younger child. It has a nice balance between remembering and having fun. We use individual pages for different children as they make good keepsakes, and this is copyright approved if not done for commercial use. It also provides advice on making a memory box (see Chapter 6).

I Have a Question about Death, *Grad Gaines, A. and Englander Polsky, M. (2017) London: Jessica Kingsley*

At last! A book that is especially helpful for those on the autism spectrum and/or with other special needs. Practitioners and families have struggled for years without a book that meets these very particular needs. There is a complete story with clear text, a short picture story for children who learn best through visual clues, and also suggestions for the adults in the child's life: 'Mostly I learned that asking questions really helps!' Factual, honest and written in a Social Story™ style.

Missing Mummy, *Cobb, R. (2011) London: Macmillan*

This emotive book deals with the death of their mother from the child's point of view. The book shows that the father is sad too. 'He wishes she was here too, but we are still a family... Together we look at photographs which make us laugh and cry...we help each other do the things Mummy used to help with. Daddy says I do them really well..' This is an honest and touching book that will help a bereaved child communicate their mixed emotions.

A Place in My Heart, *Aubrey, A. and Barton, P. (2008) London: QED Publishing*

Andrew's Grandad has died, and the story allows him to talk about his sad and confused feelings with his mum and dad. There is no big agenda here, just beautiful illustrations with a mixed heritage family. There is a very gentle exploration with Andrew about what has happened and how he remembers his Grandad. As time passes, we see Andrew playing with his friend and remembering Grandad in a loving and positive way. We think that this is a good nursery staple and perfect for early years children.

Death Is Stupid (Ordinary Terrible Things), *Higginbotham, A. (2020) New York: The Feminist Press*

'When a loved one dies...people can say some...stupid things.' Sometimes, the people around the bereaved child do not know what to say, and this book captures this very well, adding to the anger and confusion of the child in this story – hearing 'She's in a better place', for example. How do adults make sense of the senseless? We cannot, so how can we help children on the journey through their grief? You might find it useful to read this book as a staff team. You may not want to use it in nursery with the children, but you could use it as a discussion tool with your training (see Appendix C). A lesson here, wonderfully given, on telling the truth and being honest with children and working hard as the adult to empower them.

Books for adults about bereavement

This is a short list of books that we think are useful. There are many others to discover. In addition, other books are mentioned in the list of references at the end of each chapter.

Never Too Young to Grieve: Supporting Children under Five after the Death of a Parent, *Winston's Wish*

This is an excellent handbook and, we would say, another staff-room essential. The information is actually applicable to any death, not just that of a parent. Winston's Wish (see contact details in Appendix B) have other books for all ages and circumstances, including suicide and death in the armed forces. There is enough information in each book to start you thinking and planning, or to use as a crib sheet when support is needed unexpectedly.

Talking about Death, a Dialogue Between Parent and Child, *Grollman, E. (1991) Boston, MA: Beacon Press*

Sensitive and helpful advice about loss for adults working with children. Grollman shows real care and concern for children's feelings. There are useful notes for the adults, including a helpful list of 'dos' and 'don'ts '. It is a practical book, and is excellent in communicating the different understandings and awareness children have about death at different ages and stages of development. Not a long or 'heavy' read.

Michael Rosen's Sad Book, *Rosen, M. and Blake, Q. (2004) London: Walker Books*

Rosen writes from the heart about his sadness following the death of Eddie (his 19-year-old son) from meningitis and how he tries to deal with it. This heartbreaking but wonderful book crosses the ages and speaks to us all, acknowledging that sadness is not always avoidable. Quentin Blake said the picture of Michael 'being sad but trying to look happy' is the most difficult drawing he's ever done. It can be very hard to use this book with young children, but we think that this is another essential for the staff room.

Helping Children Cope with the Loss of a Loved One: A Guide for Grown Ups, *Kroen, W. (1996) Minneapolis, MN: Free Spirit Publishing*

This is a good book that covers children from birth to adolescence and explains their understanding of death at each age/stage. It is a proactive, practical approach, with advice on words to use and actions to take, this is not a long book and for some people it may even seem a bit basic. Still, it's one of our long-time favourites as a staff-room staple.

Other books for children that deal with associated loss issues in this book

Moving House, *Civardi, A. (2005) London: Usborne Books*

We found this to be slightly stereotyped around gender, but it contains useful pictures with lots of detail and is suitable for use with very young children.

Topsy and Tim Move House, *Adamson, J. (2015) London: Ladybird Books*

We thought that this could be seen as old fashioned and with a stereotypical family, but it is a simple story that opens up the conversation with very young children.

Moving Molly, *Hughes, S. (1991) London: Red Fox*

This is a well-loved favourite and is still worthy of inclusion here. It has lovely illustrations and a useful comparison of the old house with the new.

My Name is Not Refugee, *Milner, K. (2017) Edinburgh: Barrington Stoke*

Written from the viewpoint of a child refugee, this is a powerful and moving story that takes you along on the journey. What is it like leaving a country, your home, never to go back? This has great emotional impact. You could tie this in with the careful and thoughtful use of your Persona Doll (see Chapter 6), and you will be very able to inform and support all the children in nursery, whether they are refugees or not.

It's a No Money Day, *Milner, K. (2019) Edinburgh: Barrington Stoke*

'My Mum works really hard and knows lots of fun things to do that don't cost any money. But when there's nothing left in the cupboards and we have to go to the foodbank…' This is not a bereavement as such, but there is a sense of loss in this book. As well as feelings of grief there is hope, compassion and love here too. Again, use this story in conjunction with your Persona Doll to aid the children in your nursery to adopt a realistic view of the world and develop empathy. *Don't forget, ensure that you read any book first, before you read it to the children.*

Appendix B
Online resources

Childhood Bereavement UK

Helpline: 0800 02 888 40

www.childhoodbereavementuk.org

Here you will find a good example of an early years bereavement policy that includes sample letters to parents.

Gingerbread: single parents, equal families

Free helpline: 0808 802 0925

www.gingerbread.org.uk

This well-known charity offers advice to single parents after divorce and separation, and they can give advice on where to find local groups.

Letterbox Library

www.letterboxlibrary.com

In Appendix A we provide a list of some of the books that we have found helpful. We would recommend that you look at the this online bookseller as all the books have been closely vetted in order to ensure that they reflect diversity and inclusion.

Persona Dolls

www.personadolluk.org

Here you can access training and also purchase dolls with guidance on activities to do with them and how to set them up as a resource.

Sands

Free helpline: 0808 164 3332

www.sands.org.uk

helpline@sands.org.uk

This is a well-respected stillbirth and neonatal death charity that supports anyone affected by the death of a baby. Sands also works with professionals supporting the families and provides local support groups and a free helpline.

Sudden

www.suddendeath.org

This website provides online guidance for professionals and carers helping to support children who are suddenly bereaved. They also provide guidance on helping children to understand their strong emotions. Sudden also produce the 'Amy and Tom' books which are very helpful; you can download a free copy of their book for children: *Someone had Died Suddenly*. Amy and Tom, two children who have been bereaved and are grieving, narrate the story. There is simple language and good colour illustrations. This lovely resource encourages honest and straightforward dialogue between children and their carers. There is also a free downloadable guide for adults to go with the story. We suggest that this would be a good resource to print copies out for the staff room.

Winston's Wish

Freephone helpline: 08088 020 021

www.winstonswish.org

info@winstonswish.org

This charity has unique experience in assisting families affected by death through murder or terrorism. They are national experts with great credentials, and help children, families and workers dealing with any death or bereavement.

National Domestic Abuse Helpline

Domestic abuse helpline: 0808 2000 247

Refugee Council

General enquiries: 020 734 66700

info@refugeecouncil.org.uk

This is a national charity that can help track down local support/groups.

Appendix C
Delivering training sessions on loss and grief in early years to staff teams

This section examines a range of ideas and activities for in-house training with an early years staff team in a daycare setting. The main purpose of the training is to get the staff team discussing this area of early years work, and the activities we suggest are prompts in order to do this.

We have split the training programme into different stand-alone activities so that you can choose what might fit the time slot that you have available. Put together as a complete programme we would think this could be a day's training, depending on the size of the team, but we appreciate that not every staff team can get together for a whole day. Training often happens within a short team meeting at the end of a long working day, or sometimes in a morning or an afternoon. It might be that you have a training day where the morning is taken up with OFSTED briefings and items concerning the running of the setting and you have the afternoon to explore some development and training. If you are not experienced in delivering training, then starting with a smaller package of a couple of icebreakers and one main activity might be a good way in until you feel more confident. If you don't feel confident delivering this very sensitive area of training, then consider asking a more experienced colleague from your own setting or another setting to co-facilitate with you. Another option would be to arrange for an early years trainer to deliver it. Managing this training can be difficult if you are not experienced and do not feel prepared. The quote below is from a nursery manager:

> I always felt sick with nerves before a staff meeting, especially if I had to ask staff to make a change to their practice. I had come from outside and many of the staff were older and more experienced at that setting than me. I knew there would be opposition to my ideas and one person especially would question the reason for change while others would just sit there with their arms folded and their coats on making it clear from their expressions that they didn't agree with me. After I went

on training and learnt to breathe deeply before speaking and other techniques for calming myself I felt much better. I learn some phrases to say to help me contain the person who over contributed and encourage those who didn't more. I think the staff sensed the change in me and I got feedback that they were more confident in my decisions and less worried that I didn't know what I was doing.

(Price and Ota, 2014, p. 60)

If cost is an issue you could think about getting together with some other settings in order to make it more affordable. Your local council early years team should be able to put you in touch with a suitable trainer. It's important that the staff team feel relaxed, and that the leader of the training is aware of the depth of material in the training and is able to manage the group effectively.

We are both very familiar with early years settings and understand the time constraints that they operate under. There is often very little time when the whole team can gather together, especially when the setting is open for long hours and there are different staff shifts within this. So much of the team's time can be taken up with discussing details about the practical day-to-day running of a setting, e.g. legal briefings, issues to do with admission, new children, room and staff organisation and rotas, updating of policies and procedures, health/safety and safeguarding issues, budgetary spending and constraints, introduction of new staff and trainees – the list is endless.

However, it is very important to remember that the setting is not just a machine that has to function efficiently. It is also a place where children are cared for and educated and where their developmental and emotional needs are met. The management and wider staff team need to think about the philosophy of childcare and education that the setting delivers, as well as the way that it is managed on a practical level. We would ask you to think of the mission statement for the setting and consider whether the ethos of the setting supports this statement and delivers it. The setting needs to have a purpose and aims for its development whilst also functioning as a business. We would argue that both aspects of the setting – practical and theoretical – need to work well, and so there needs to be time for staff development in terms of childcare philosophy as well as management strategies.

This is where thinking about grief and loss is imperative as part of a whole staff training programme and shouldn't be relegated to something that is considered only when there is a crisis or difficulty. Ideally, a setting manager needs to understand that the nursery or pre-school will only run effectively and be able to deliver high-quality services to the families that use it when the ethos of the setting is fully understood and adhered to by all of the staff team. They not only have to understand it but subscribe to it as well. When this happens, the team will work more effectively as they have a shared purpose and common understanding that working in the setting is about more than just the mechanics of a provision, and that there is a core of childcare and education principles that the provision subscribes to that is at the root of all practical decisions.

It is easy to get caught up in the (very important) details of staff rotas and personalities, food and drink provision, resources and activities, cleaning and safety, liaison with parents and carers, inspections and requirements for minimum levels of vocational training – again, the list is endless. However, there has to be something underpinning this to pull it all together and make it more than the sum of its parts.

We think that by looking at feelings and how they are expressed in terms of loss and grief a cornerstone of good practice in a setting is reached. If this emotional dynamic is working effectively the setting becomes a caring and nurturing place for children, staff teams and the families who use the provision, and this should support the ethos and mission statement. The effect of this can spread to many other areas of the nursery or pre-school. We think that if you view the emotional work as essential rather than as an add-on in terms of training, you will see the benefits of it in staff relationships with each other, and with children and families.

We would suggest giving participants advance notice of the training. This is so that they can prepare themselves for what might be a an emotional or triggering session for them. Louise Rowling refers to 'layers of protection' (Rowling, 2003, p. 169), the third of which is to forewarn.

Students have the option of not being involved. A similar process is adopted in the class. They can pass on activities and are not forced to be involved in discussions. (p169). We cover the other layers within our outline.

As always, at the beginning of training we would talk about housekeeping (people like to know what time they will have breaks), any access or other needs anyone has, any rules (e.g. one person speaking at a time, phones off and away) and confidentiality. This is especially important in this training, as people have to feel that they can trust the group. Of course, there might be talk afterwards about the concepts and messages of the training – indeed, we hope that there will be. However, this is different from ascribing remarks to individuals or gossiping about people's responses.

Icebreakers

We continue this session outline with some ideas for icebreakers and fun warm-ups. You might only use a couple of these if your staff team is well established and close. However, don't skip these to get to the 'real' issues, especially if you have time constraints. It's very important to start with a short period where the team can relax and focus on where they are and what they are going to do. If you start the main activities straight away many people will take a while to engage with them, as they will still be thinking about everything they came into the room with. They need this time to really be present at the training.

The second purpose of the icebreakers is to ease the team together if they don't know each other that well or if they rarely get together as a whole group. It might be that there are some new staff members or people who have taken on new roles within the setting. Whatever the situation, it is likely that they will not be used to looking at such a sensitive subject in this kind of depth. Some of these activities ask the participants to be quite personally revealing and open. This can't happen in a team who don't trust each other. Of course, a couple of icebreaker activities are not going to pull together a staff team who have serious issues, and we would ask you to think carefully about embarking on such training if in this situation. In such cases, it might be better to work on team building before trying this work.

The third purpose of the icebreakers is to convey some of the ideas that underpin the training on loss and grief. Using names, knowing about other team members, being able to work with a wide variety of people – these are all important skills that practitioners need in order to deal with sensitive topics such as grief and loss. They are also skills that we need to model for children so that they can see how to use them effectively. Only a close and trusting team can talk honestly and openly about their feelings in a professional way. If children sense this unity, they will also feel more inclined to trust the adults around them and open up about their own feelings.

Finally, these activities mix people within the group, as they are very likely to come into the training room and sit with their friends or other familiar colleagues. In our experience of whole team training, there are groups of people who rarely interact with each other. For example, the staff team from the baby room may never talk to or engage with the team from the rising fives room. The older staff members may rarely talk to younger ones, new staff might find it hard to break into groups with established friendships, and so on. These are great activities to suggest that people are going to have to mix and get to know team members who may be unfamiliar to them. We would recommend returning to icebreakers after every intermission so that the team continues to mix and work with people they might not know so well. This can take up to ten minutes depending on the size of the team (that's the average length of an icebreaker).

Icebreakers: Part 1

Using names

I was talking to a Polish early years practitioner and we were discussing her background, where she lived and when she came to the UK. I commented that Judy (her name) wasn't a Polish name that I knew. She replied 'Oh, that's not my actual name, but when I came here they all said that they couldn't say my real name,

Jadwiga, and so they called me Judy. I was the new girl and I was already different as I had an accent so I didn't want to cause any more problems.'

Reflections

I wonder if the staff team in this story would have allowed this same behaviour with a new child in their setting? It can be embarrassing and worrying if we can't pronounce someone's name the first time that we hear it. However, it *is* their name and we have to make an effort until we get it right. Acknowledging with the person concerned that we need to practice can be a lighter way of continuing to repeat the name and check with the person when we have succeeded. Taken to the extreme, staff members who feel embarrassed that they can't say someone's name might avoid that person so that they don't have to say their name.

We want children to mix with each other and to know each other's names. In order to do that we have to be role models for them and show them that we work as a whole team. Helping children to have this kind of flexibility and the ability to get on with each other, ask someone's name and keep asking until they understand it, and work with lots of different children is a great gift and works well in terms of sharing feelings and gaining support.

There is another point to the random grouping and pairing activities that we use in training sessions that shows more fully why we use them. Many of us remember the agony of being at school and having team leaders pick their team members. This might be a pleasant memory for you if you were generally a team leader, or if you were popular and good at sports. However, if you were always one of the last to be selected this could have been a humiliating and upsetting experience, and we would not wish this practice to continue in early years and primary settings.

Another strategy teachers sometimes use that appears to be more user friendly is to say to children 'Get into two's' or 'Find a friend to stand next to'. We would suggest that this way of grouping also puts pressure on those children who do not have a friend, or who have more than one friend and don't know which one to pick. Being sensitive to the feelings of children at this level will ensure more sensitive interaction with them when thinking about grief and loss.

(1) Sitting or standing in a circle the team introduce themselves and then introduce the person on each side of them. This is a very quick activity to get everyone to check on names and make sure that people know the names of those either side of them, at least.
(2) Ask the group to sit or stand in a circle. Make a gap on your right then say 'There's a space on my right and I would like (name of someone) to stand over here'. This creates a space on someone else's right and they have to do the same thing, and so it continues. Explain that if they don't know someone's name they can ask them.

Make sure that everyone has a go. This is good for getting to know, remembering and practicing names.

(3) Ask the group to sit or stand in a circle. Start by saying your name and a word that describes you starting with the first letter of your name, for example 'My name is Deborah and I am delicious'. The whole group has to repeat this: 'Her name's Deborah and she is delicious'. Again, this is a good one for remembering names. You can also do this by using a gesture instead of a word. As in 'I'm Deborah' (curtseys)' and everyone says 'She's Deborah' (and curtseys)

Icebreakers: Part 2

Finding out about each other

(1) Get people to line up (in silence) in order of their house number (ask them to say it when the line is completed in order to check that the task has been executed correctly). Move on to using their birthday month to line up (again, ask them to reveal this). Finally, use the first initial of their middle name. This is all done in silence and relies on people miming, making hand gestures (perhaps Makaton?) and helping each other if they can see that someone is in the wrong place. After this last activity, ask them to say their middle name and where it came from. Were they named after a relative? If someone doesn't have a middle name then they could think of a middle name that they would like to have. This is a fun activity involving personal details that gets people moving around and revealing a little bit about themselves.

(2) In pairs (taken randomly from the activity above or another activity), allow a few minutes to find out three things about each other. None of these can be that they work in early years. Suggestions we use are 'What did you want to be when you were little', 'Where did you last go on holiday?', 'What other jobs have you done' or 'What is something we might not know about you'. Once back in the circle, the pairs introduce each other: 'This is my friend Clair and she…'

(3) Get the group to stand in a huddle. Ask them to get into smaller groups according to what they had for breakfast. You can start the activity by putting your hand up and say 'Toast over here'. When they are in groups you can go round and ask what they all had for breakfast. You can alter this by getting them into groups by their favourite chocolate bar, drink, etc.

Extended icebreaker: Finding out more about each other

The following activity works as an icebreaker, but it takes longer and the reflections afterwards feed directly into the grief and loss work, so we would suggest doing this after the quicker icebreakers.

Put people into pairs (a three is possible if odd numbers)

Give them each a sheet that has a list of questions on it (we suggest no more than ten) and a pen. These questions rely on how well they know each other. If it is a close team then you might have to devise your own questions. Examples we have used are:

What is their favourite food?
Do they have a pet? What kind?
What is their favourite colour?
What would they drink on a night out?
Where would they like to go on holiday?
What's their favourite television programme?
Do they like Marmite?
What hobbies do they have?
If it rains do they use an umbrella or a hat?
Where in the world would they like to live if not in the UK?
Who was their idol where they were younger?
What kind of music do they like?

Tell the team members that they are going to answer these questions about the other person in the pair WITHOUT asking their partner and in silence. There is usually a sense of bewilderment here – how are we going to do that? You then say that you are going to answer the questions by

1. Thinking about what you already know about them
2. Looking at them
3. Guessing

It is important to stress that this is a fun activity; perhaps say to the group before they start, 'let's make a group pact not to get upset or offended at any of the answers'. When they have filled in their sheet they can give it to the other person and see how many they have right. There is usually a lot of laughing, astonishment and perhaps mild outrage at the results.

After the amusement has died down and you regroup, you can raise the following points:

- The point of this exercise is not the answers that were given but how they were arrived at – ask the team how they got their answers and if they were accurate or way off the mark.

- You can suggest that we devise the answers by making assumptions about our partner, based on what we know already about them, by looking at them and by guessing.

- We might also make assumptions because of their age (especially for the last two questions).
- We might make cultural assumptions.
- We might just assume that they like exactly the same kind of things we do.

This is fine in a fun activity such as this as there are no consequences to our assumptions. However, when we are working with children and families we should not make assumptions without checking. In terms of this book, we cannot assume that the family has the same attitudes to grief and loss that we have. It's really important when working in early years that we continually self-audit our thinking and responses so that we don't make assumptions about children and families based on their gender, class or cultural background. An obvious example is 'Oh, he won't want to play with that because he is a boy'. In terms of grief and loss it might be 'Of course they won't be taking the child to the funeral', because that's not what we'd choose to do. We should always check to see if the assumption that we are making is true or not by asking the child or the parent. That is because our assumptions may lead to actions, and actions have consequences.

Main training activities

These main activities are fluid in terms of duration; it depends on the size of the group and the discussion that arises. The activities are basically prompts for further discussions. We believe that the team has all of the requisite knowledge and skills between them already, and this training is designed to bring their attributes to the fore. There might be some information or resources that will be useful, but the main aim is to get discussion going and talk about how we relate to children in terms of feelings about grief and loss. The crucial point is that we cannot relate to children before we have thought about our own attitudes, beliefs and feelings.

These activities are very personal, so it is important that people are aware that they can 'pass' if they don't want to share something with the group. The activities can bring up all sorts of emotions and feelings. It can be helpful to make yourself available at the end of the training to talk to anyone who wants to do so. The other thing we used to do when delivering this training was to finish a little early, possibly 30 minutes or so. We would then say to the students that this was 'free' time and not to go rushing off to their next commitments. No one was expecting them home or back at work for this timeslot and it was a perfect gift of time we were giving them in order to go and have a walk or a coffee and just relax after what can be quite a gruelling session.

Activity 1 (this can take up to an hour)

Personal experiences of grief and loss

In pairs, ask them to talk about their first experience of death as a child. This could be a pet, a relation or a neighbour, perhaps. Give as much detail as possible. What was actually said to them? What happened in terms of funerals or memorials?

After this, assemble the team in a circle and ask them to share if they feel able to. Then put them into different pairs. What would they say to a child if they were asked about death? What actual words would they use? Ask the team to reassemble in a circle and share this too. If you can, put these responses on to a flip chart.

Reflections on this activity

As adults, and as early years practitioners, we want to spare children feelings of sadness and grief. As we have noted, this can lead us to minimise their feelings or try and quash them. We want to protect children and keep them happy, but sometimes that is not possible. What we have to do in terms of these feelings (especially with bereavement) is:

- Liaise with the parents and carers. Whatever our beliefs are and whatever words we would use to a child, we have to ensure that we are following the parents' wishes. For example, we might believe in heaven but they might not.

- We don't have to respond there and then. If we rush to answer, we may not be offering the child suitable support. We can say 'That's a very interesting question and I'm going to have a bit of a think, but I will talk to you again at…(say a specific time)'.

- We need to be cautious in our responses and only give the child the information they have asked for.

- We need to let children be sad and upset if they want to and not try to distract them or quell them.

- However, we also need to make sure that we don't expect sadness or suggest feelings to children that they may not have.

Activity 2

We suggest using some of the scenarios that we have detailed throughout this book in order to further explore 'What would I do' discussions. The way that we have structured this is to have small groups of three or four people who look at a scenario and then write some suggestions for what they would do. It's good to have a large piece of paper for the scenarios and the suggestions. You can then move the scenarios around so that every group can see all of them. You can also share the suggestions so that each group can see if their suggestions were similar.

Activity 3

Society and death and loss

This will need some research on your part. You will need to have a look at different cultural practices in terms of death and have a group discussion about them. If you have a staff member who practices a particular faith you cannot assume that they will have detailed knowledge of this specific practice. There are many different ways of being Jewish, Muslim, Christian, Sikh, Hindu, Buddhist, etc., and we need to ensure that we explore a wide range of diverse practices and attitudes to death and loss.

There can also be discussion about age here, and whether this affects attitudes to death and loss. We can talk about the idea that children should be 'seen and not heard', how this has changed, and what this means in terms of supporting a child with their feelings.

We can discuss gender too, and think about whether this has any bearing on the way that adults respond to children and also their expectations of children. An example of this is expecting boys not to cry, or girls to be more emotional.

Finally, what about class? Is there an idea of a 'stiff upper lip' and is this class based? Is there a working class idea of 'mustn't grumble, I just have to get on with things and not ask for help'?

Activity 4

Resources

Here we would suggest that you collate all of the resources that you have that might support this type of work. We would include ideas for activities that look at feelings, books, DVDs, toys, etc. Use the resource lists we have provided to think about what you have in terms of usefulness and diversity. Then, start to compile a 'wish list' and think about a date by which you can achieve it. You might ask for volunteers from each room in the setting to think about suitable activities that would encourage children to talk about their feelings. You need to have a timescale for this in order to ensure that it happens. We would suggest setting a deadline for the volunteers to report back on what they have done and how it went. They could present it as a verbal report or compile it into a display. What about parents and carers? You could let them know that you will be focusing on this type of work in the setting. You might use a newsletter for this or another form of suitable communication.

Final activities

We always find it useful to have some kind of final evaluation to pull the session together and help people reflect on what they have achieved. It might be that everyone stands by a picture that represents how they feel (you would need to find a good range of pictures for this). Or you could go round and ask them to say one thing that they've found useful and one thing they might do differently as a result of the training. You might use a more formal written evaluation, although we find that at the end of a busy training session people aren't at their most receptive to sitting and writing, so a more quick-fire sample of their responses might be best now, with more reflective feedback at a later date.

Remembrance

At the end of a session, we like to spend a moment thinking of those who have died. Again, it's important that no one feels pressured into doing this; people are always welcome to pass. We stand in a circle and either light a tea light and put it on a tray, saying the name of the person we are remembering (or not, as preferred). If there are concerns about naked flames, another option is for each person to take a sprig of rosemary from a bowl and keep it to take away with them. Rosemary is a herb that is traditionally used to signify remembrance. We have found this to be a lovely, reflective way to end a training session on grief and loss.

We hope that you have found these suggestions for training sessions useful and that you are able to tailor them to your own team's requirements and needs. The whole session does fit together quite well, but if you didn't have time for all of this, we would suggest a couple of icebreakers followed by one of the main activities and finally the remembrance activity. This would be a good mini session. The main aim is to get people talking and to pull the team closer together. If they are able to talk to each other about their own feelings in the controlled environment of a staff training session, then they are more likely to be able to talk to parents, carers and children about their feelings.

References

Price, D., & Ota, C. (2014) *Leading and Supporting Early Years Teams: A Practical Guide*. Abingdon: Routledge.

Rowling, L. (2003) *Grief in School Communities: Effective Support Strategies*. Buckingham: Open University Press.

Index

For Product Safety Concerns and Information please contact our EU
representative GPSR@taylorandfrancis.com
Taylor & Francis Verlag GmbH, Kaufingerstraße 24, 80331 München, Germany

www.ingramcontent.com/pod-product-compliance
Lightning Source LLC
Chambersburg PA
CBHW081436270326
41932CB00019B/3225

9 780367 422974